THE MOUNTAIN BIKER'S GUIDE TO

NORTHERN CALIFORNIA AND NEVADA

Dennis Coello's America by Mountain Bike Series

THE MOUNTAIN BIKER'S GUIDE TO
NORTHERN CALIFORNIA AND NEVADA

Dennis Coello's America by
Mountain Bike Series

Aimée Serrurier

Foreword, Introduction, and Afterword
by Dennis Coello, Series Editor

MENASHA
RIDGE
PRESS

FALCON™

Library of Congress Cataloging-in-Publication Data
Serrurier, Aimée:
  The mountain biker's guide to northern California and
Nevada / Aimée Serrurier : foreword, introduction, and
afterword by Dennis Coello.—1st ed.
    p.   cm.
  —(Dennis Coello's America by mountain bike series)
  ISBN 1-56044-218-2
  1. All terrain cycling—California, Northern—Guidebooks.
2. All terrain cycling—Nevada—Guidebooks. 3. California,
Northern—Guidebooks. 4. Nevada—Guidebooks. I. Title.
II. Series: America by mountain bike series.
GV1045.5.C22C257   1994
796.6'4'09794—dc20   94-6466
                                        CIP

Photos by the author unless otherwise credited
Maps by Tim Krasnansky
Cover photo by Dennis Coello

Menasha Ridge Press
3169 Cahaba Heights Road
Birmingham, Alabama 35243

Falcon Press
P.O. Box 1718
Helena, Montana 59624

 Text pages printed on recycled paper.

Table of Contents

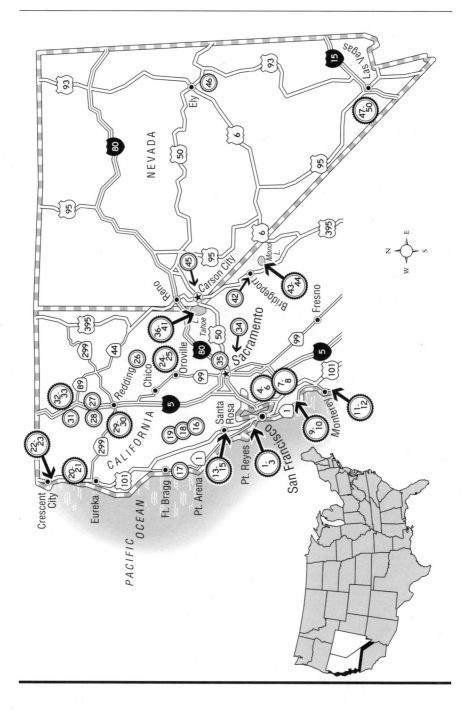

List of Maps

AMERICA BY MOUNTAIN BIKE *MAP LEGEND*

Ride trailhead

Steep grade

Primary bike trail

Direction of travel

(arrows point downhill)

Optional bike trail and trailhead

Other trail

Hiking trail

Interstate highways (with exit no.)

U.S. routes

State routes

Lagunitas Rd.

Other paved roads

Unpaved, gravel or dirt roads (may be 4WD only)

U.S. Forest Service roads

Sacramento ◉
Reno

Cities

Clear Lake ◉
Weaverville

Towns or settlements

Dam

Lake

River, stream or canal

0   ½   1

MILES

Approximate scale in miles

N

True North

REDWOOD PARK

Parklands

State Border

✈ Airport

♥ Archeological or historical site

▲ Campground (CG)

≡ Cattle guard

⌘ Cemetery or gravesite

⛪ Church

Cliff, escarpment or outcropping

Drinking water

Fire tower or lookout

🔲 Food

Gate

House or cabin

Lodging

Mountain or butte

Mountain pass

△ Mountain summit
3312 (elevation in feet)

Military test site

✕ Mine or quarry

Museum

Observatory

Park office or ranger station

Picnic area

Power line or pipeline

Restrooms

Ranch or horse farm

Ski Area

Swimming Area

Transmission towers

Tunnel or bridge

Foreword

Welcome to *America by Mountain Bike,* a 20-book series designed to provide all-terrain bikers with the information they need to find and ride the very best trails everywhere in the mainland United States. Whether you're new to the sport and don't know where to pedal, or an experienced mountain biker who wants to learn the classic trails in another region, this series is for you. Drop a few bucks for the book, spend an hour with the detailed maps and route descriptions, and you're prepared for the finest in off-road cycling.

My role as editor of this series was simple: First, find a mountain biker who knows the area and loves to ride. Second, ask that person to spend a year researching the most popular and very best rides around. And third, have that rider describe each trail in terms of difficulty, scenery, condition, elevation change, and all other categories of information that are important to trail riders. "Pretend you've just completed a ride and met up with fellow mountain bikers at the trailhead," I told each author. "Imagine their questions, be clear in your answers."

As I said, the *editorial* process—that of sending out riders and reading the submitted chapters—is a snap. But the work involved in finding, riding, and writing about each trail is enormous. In some instances our authors' tasks are made easier by the information contributed by local bike shops or cycling clubs, or even by the writers of local "where-to" guides. Credit for these contributions is provided, when appropriate, in each chapter, and our sincere thanks goes to all who have helped.

But the overwhelming majority of trails are discovered and pedaled by our authors themselves, then compared with dozens of other routes to determine if they qualify as "classic"—that area's best in scenery and cycling fun. If you've ever had the experience of pioneering a route from outdated topographic maps, or entering a bike shop to request information from local riders who would much prefer to keep their favorite trails secret, or know how it is to double- and triple-check data to be positive your trail info is correct, then you have an idea of how each of our authors has labored to bring about these books. You and I, and all the mountain bikers of America, are the richer for their efforts.

You'll get more out of this book if you take a moment to read the Introduction explaining how to read the trail listings. The "Topographic Maps" section will help you understand how useful topos will be on a ride, and will also tell you where to get them. And though this is a "where-to," not a "how-to" guide, those of you who have not traveled the backcountry might find the planning and equipment tips in "Hitting the Trail" of particular value.

In addition to the material above, newcomers to mountain biking might want to spend a minute with the glossary, page 171, so that terms like *hardpack*, *single-track*, and *water bars* won't throw you when you come across them in the text.

Finally, the tips in the Afterword on mountain biking etiquette and the land-use controversy might help us all enjoy the trails a little more.

All the best.

Dennis Coello
Salt Lake City

Preface

Northern California and Nevada have some of the best mountain biking terrain in the country. From glacial peaks to coastal hills, from wide-open valleys to desert canyons and forested foothills, this region contains a variety of trails. Tame bike paths, rolling fire trails, and challenging single-tracks combine to make Northern California and Nevada a paradise for mountain bikers of all abilities. Beginner, intermediate, and advanced fat-tire buffs will find a plethora of trails to choose from, many within the borders of recreation areas and county, state, and national forests.

Contained within this book are fifty rides. To the north, along the Oregon border, a challenging ride circumnavigates the slopes of Mount Shasta. Other rides north of San Francisco zigzag through the wine country out to the coast and through the redwoods. South of "The City," fire trails weave in and out of county and state parks as far south as Monterey. To the east, scenic bike trails wind along the Sacramento River. Still farther east, challenging single-track trails showcase the breathtaking beauty of sparkling Lake Tahoe.

In Nevada, seven diverse rides, including one in the Lake Tahoe area, are scattered across the state. Starting with the eastern shores of Lake Tahoe, mountain trails explore the scenery above the lake and around Carson City. Moving toward the rising sun, we check out our second-newest national park, Great Basin. Although there is no off-road riding in the park, the paved and unpaved roads running through its diverse terrain of steep hills and desert valleys make it a mountain bike mecca. Surprisingly enough, there are more great rides to be found not far outside the city limits of Las Vegas.

Many of the trails described in this guide can be ridden year-round. In each description, I've indicated the best months for riding, but it's sound practice to always check the local weather report before attempting a ride. Be prepared for all kinds of weather by bringing appropriate clothing and food.

Most of these rides are near either small towns or urban areas, where accommodations range from campgrounds to five-star hotels. Basic services such as groceries, gas, and coffee shops usually are available nearby. For your convenience, I've listed the local bike shops in each area. These folks are your best resource for getting current information about trail conditions and recent developments, such as newly opened or closed trails. They also can point you to the best coffee shop in town and supply you with spare parts, additional maps, and further directions.

Many thanks to John Burke (Buggy), who introduced me to mountain biking originally and later to Mount Tamalpais and the Marin headlands. If you have any questions about bikes or trails, you can find him at Noe Valley Cyclery in San Francisco.

Aimée Serrurier

Introduction

Information on each trail in this book begins with a general description that includes length, configuration, scenery, highlights, trail conditions, and difficulty. Additional description is contained in eleven individual categories. The following will help you understand all of the information provided.

Trail name: Trail names are as designated on United States Geological Survey (USGS) or Forest Service or other maps, and/or by local custom.

Length: The overall length of a trail is described in miles, unless stated otherwise.

Configuration: This is a description of the shape of each trail—whether the trail is a loop, out-and-back (that is, along the same route), figure eight, trapezoid, isosceles triangle, or if it connects with another trail described in the book.

Difficulty: This provides at a glance a description of the degree of physical exertion required to complete the ride, and the technical skill required to pedal it. Authors were asked to keep in mind the fact that all riders are not equal, and thus to gauge the trail in terms of how the middle-of-the-road rider—someone between the newcomer and Ned Overend—could handle the route. Comments about the trail's length, condition, and elevation change will also assist you in determining the difficulty of any trail relative to your own abilities.

Condition: Trails are described in terms of being paved, unpaved, sandy, hard-packed, washboarded, two- or four-wheel-drive, single-track or double-track. All terms that might be unfamiliar to the first-time mountain biker are defined in the Glossary.

Scenery: Here you will find a general description of the natural surroundings during the seasons most riders pedal the trail, and a suggestion of what is to be found at special times (like great fall foliage or cactus in bloom).

Highlights: Towns, major water crossings, historical sites, etc., are listed.

General location: This category describes where the trail is located in reference to a nearby town or other landmark.

Elevation change: Unless stated otherwise, the figure provided is the total gain and loss of elevation along the trail. In regions where the elevation variation is not extreme, the route is simply described as flat, rolling, or possessing short steep climbs or descents.

Season: This is the best time of year to pedal the route, taking into account trail

1

condition (for example, when it will not be muddy), riding comfort (when the weather is too hot, cold, or wet), and local hunting seasons.

Note: Because the exact opening and closing dates of deer, elk, moose, and antelope seasons often change from year to year, riders should check with the local Fish and Game department, or call a sporting goods store (or any place that sells hunting licenses) in a nearby town before heading out. Wear bright clothes in fall, and don't wear suede jackets while in the saddle. Hunter's-orange tape on the helmet is also a good idea.

Services: This category is of primary importance in guides for paved-road tourers, but is far less crucial to most mountain bike trail descriptions because there are usually no services whatsoever to be found. Authors have noted when water is available on desert or long mountain routes, and have listed the availability of food, lodging, campgrounds, and bike shops. If all these services are present, you will find only the words "All services available in . . ."

Hazards: Special hazards like steep cliffs, great amounts of deadfall, or barbed-wire fences very close to the trail are noted here.

Rescue Index: Determining how far one is from help on any particular trail can be difficult due to the backcountry nature of most mountain bike rides. Authors therefore state the proximity of homes or Forest Service outposts, nearby roads where one might hitch a ride, or the likelihood of other bikers being encountered on the trail. Phone numbers of local sheriff departments or hospitals have not been provided because phones are almost never available. If you are able to reach a phone, the local operator will connect you with emergency services.

Land Status: This category provides information regarding whether the trail crosses land operated by the Forest Service, Bureau of Land Management, a city, state, or national park, whether it crosses private land whose owner (at the time the author did the research) has allowed mountain bikers right of passage, and so on.

Note: Authors have been extremely careful to offer only those routes that are open to bikers and are legal to ride. However, because land ownership changes over time, and because the land-use controversy created by mountain bikes still has not completely subsided, it is the duty of each cyclist to look for and to heed signs warning against trail use. Don't expect this book to get you off the hook when you're facing some small-town judge for pedaling past a "Biking Prohibited" sign erected the day before. Look for these signs, read them, and heed the advice. And remember there's always another trail.

Maps: The maps in this book have been produced with great care, and, in conjunction with the trail-following suggestions, will help you stay on course. But as every experienced mountain biker knows, things can get tricky in the backcountry. It is therefore strongly suggested that you avail yourself of the detailed information found in the 7.5 minute series USGS (United States Geological Survey) topographic maps. In some cases, authors have found that specific Forest Service or other maps may be more useful than the USGS quads, and tell how to obtain them.

Finding the trail: Detailed information on how to reach the trailhead, and where to park your car is provided here.

Sources of additional information: Here you will find the address and/or phone number of a bike shop, governmental agency, or other source from which trail information can be obtained.

Notes on the trail: This is where you are guided carefully through any portions of the trail that are particularly difficult to follow. The author also may add information about the route that does not fit easily into the other categories. This category will not be present for those rides where the route is easy to follow.

ABBREVIATIONS

The following road-designation abbreviations are used in the *America by Mountain Bike* series:

CR	County Road
FR	Farm Route
FS	Forest Service road
I-	Interstate
IR	Indian Route
US	United States highway

State highways are designated with the appropriate two-letter state abbreviation, followed by the road number. *Example:* UT 6 = Utah State Highway 6.

Postal Service two-letter state codes:

AL	Alabama	KY	Kentucky
AK	Alaska	LA	Louisiana
AZ	Arizona	ME	Maine
AR	Arkansas	MD	Maryland
CA	California	MA	Massachusetts
CO	Colorado	MI	Michigan
CT	Connecticut	MN	Minnesota
DE	Delaware	MS	Mississippi
DC	District of Columbia	MO	Missouri
FL	Florida	MT	Montana
GA	Georgia	NE	Nebraska
HI	Hawaii	NV	Nevada
ID	Idaho	NH	New Hampshire
IL	Illinois	NJ	New Jersey
IN	Indiana	NM	New Mexico
IA	Iowa	NY	New York
KS	Kansas	NC	North Carolina

ND	North Dakota	TX	Texas
OH	Ohio	UT	Utah
OK	Oklahoma	VT	Vermont
OR	Oregon	VA	Virginia
PA	Pennsylvania	WA	Washington
RI	Rhode Island	WV	West Virginia
SC	South Carolina	WI	Wisconsin
SD	South Dakota	WY	Wyoming
TN	Tennessee		

TOPOGRAPHIC MAPS

The maps in this book, when used in conjunction with the route directions present in each chapter, will in most instances be sufficient to get you to the trail and keep you on it. However, you will find superior detail and valuable information in the 7.5-minute series United States Geological Survey (USGS) topographic maps. Recognizing how indispensable these are to bikers and hikers alike, many bike shops and sporting goods stores now carry topos of the local area.

But if you're brand new to mountain biking you might be wondering "What's a topographic map?" In short, these differ from standard "flat" maps in that they indicate not only linear distance, but elevation as well. One glance at a "topo" will show you the difference, for "contour lines" are spread across the map like dozens of intricate spider webs. Each contour line represents a particular elevation, and at the base of each topo a particular "contour interval" designation is given. Yes, it sounds confusing if you're new to the lingo, but it truly is a simple and wonderfully helpful system. Keep reading.

Let's assume that the 7.5-minute series topo before us says "Contour Interval 40 feet," and that the short trail we'll be pedaling is two inches in length on the map, and that it crosses five contour lines from beginning to end. What do we know? Well, because the linear scale of this series is 2,000 feet to the inch (roughly 2¾ inches representing 1 mile), we know our trail is approximately ⅘ of a mile long (2 inches × 2,000 feet). But we also know we'll be climbing or descending 200 vertical feet (5 contour lines × 40 feet each) over that distance. And the elevation designations written on occasional contour lines will tell us if we're heading up or down.

The authors of this series warn their readers of upcoming terrain, but only a detailed topo gives you the information you need to pinpoint your position exactly on a map, steer you toward optional trails and roads nearby, plus let you know at a glance if you'll be pedaling hard to take them. It's a lot of information for a very low cost. In fact, the only drawback with topos is their size—several feet square. I've tried rolling them into tubes, folding them carefully, even cutting them into blocks and photocopying the pieces. Any of these systems is a pain, but no matter how you pack the maps you'll be happy they're along. And you'll be even happier if you pack a compass as well.

In addition to local bike shops and sporting goods stores, you'll find topos at major universities and some public libraries, where you might try photocopying the ones you need to avoid the cost of buying them. But if you want your own and can't find them locally, write to:

USGS Map Sales
Box 25286
Denver, CO 80225

Ask for an index while you're at it, plus a price list and a copy of the booklet *Topographic Maps*. In minutes you'll be reading them like a pro.

A second excellent series of maps available to mountain bikers is that put out by the United States Forest Service. If your trail runs through an area designated as a national forest, look in the phone book (white pages) under the United States Government listings, find the Department of Agriculture heading, and then run your finger down that section until you find the Forest Service. Give them a call and they'll provide the address of the regional Forest Service office, from which you can obtain the appropriate map.

TRAIL ETIQUETTE

Pick up almost any mountain bike magazine these days and you'll find articles and letters to the editor about trail conflict. For example, you'll find hikers' tales of being blindsided by speeding mountain bikers, complaints from bikers about being blamed for trail damage that was really caused by horse or cattle traffic, and cries from bikers about those "kamikaze" riders who through their antics threaten to close even more trails to all of us.

The authors of this series have been very careful to guide you to only those trails that are open to mountain biking (or at least were open at the time of their research), and without exception have warned of the damage done to our sport through injudicious riding. My personal views on this matter appear in the Afterword, but all of us can benefit from glancing over the following International Mountain Bicycling Association (IMBA) Rules of the Trail before saddling up.

1. *Ride on open trails only.* Respect trail and road closures (ask if not sure), avoid possible trespass on private land, obtain permits and authorization as may be required. Federal and State wilderness areas are closed to cycling.

2. *Leave no trace.* Be sensitive to the dirt beneath you. Even on open trails, you should not ride under conditions where you will leave evi-

dence of your passing, such as on certain soils shortly after a rain. Observe the different types of soils and trail construction; practice low-impact cycling. This also means staying on the trail and not creating any new ones. Be sure to pack out at least as much as you pack in.

3. *Control your bicycle!* Inattention for even a second can cause disaster. Excessive speed can maim and threaten people; there is no excuse for it!

4. *Always yield the trail.* Make known your approach well in advance. A friendly greeting (or a bell) is considerate and works well; startling someone may cause loss of trail access. Show your respect when passing others by slowing to a walk or even stopping. Anticipate that other trail users may be around corners or in blind spots.

5. *Never spook animals.* All animals are startled by an unannounced approach, a sudden movement, or a loud noise. This can be dangerous for you, for others, and for the animals. Give animals extra room and time to adjust to you. In passing, use special care and follow the directions of horseback riders (ask if uncertain). Running cattle and disturbing wild animals is a serious offense. Leave gates as you found them, or as marked.

6. *Plan ahead.* Know your equipment, your ability, and the area in which you are riding—and prepare accordingly. Be self-sufficient at all times. Wear a helmet, keep your machine in good condition, and carry necessary supplies for changes in weather or other conditions. A well-executed trip is a satisfaction to you and not a burden or offense to others.

For more information, contact IMBA, P.O. Box 412043, Los Angeles, CA 90041, (818) 792-8830.

HITTING THE TRAIL

Once again, because this is a "where-to," not a "how-to" guide, the following will be brief. If you're a veteran trail rider these suggestions might serve to remind you of something you've forgotten to pack. If you're a newcomer, they might convince you to think twice before hitting the backcountry unprepared.

Water: I've heard the questions dozens of times. "How much is enough? One bottle? Two? Three?! But think of all that extra weight!" Well, one simple physiological fact should convince you to err on the side of excess when it comes to deciding how much water to pack: a human working hard in 90-degree temperature needs approximately ten quarts of fluids every day. Ten quarts. That's two and a half gallons—*12* large water bottles, or *16* small ones. And, with water weighing in at approximately 8 pounds per gallon, a one-day supply comes to a whopping 20 pounds.

In other words, pack along two or three bottles even for short rides. And make sure you can purify the water found along the trail on longer routes. When writing of those routes where this could be of critical importance, each author has provided information on where water can be found near the trail—if it can be found at all. But drink it untreated and you run the risk of disease. (See *Giardia* in the Glossary.)

One sure way to kill both the bacteria and viruses in water is to boil it for ten minutes, plus one minute more for each 1,000 feet of elevation above sea level. Right. That's just how you want to spend your time on a bike ride. Besides, who wants to carry a stove, or denude the countryside stoking bonfires to boil water?

Luckily, there is a better way. Many riders pack along the effective, inexpensive, and only slightly distasteful tetraglycine hydroperiodide tablets (sold under the names Potable Aqua, Globaline, and Coughlan's, among others). Some invest in portable, lightweight purifiers that filter out the crud. Yes, purifying water with tablets or filters is a bother. But catch a case of Giardia sometime and you'll understand why it's worth the trouble.

Tools: Ever since my first cross-country tour in 1965 I've been kidded about the number of tools I pack on the trail. And so I will exit entirely from this discussion by providing a list compiled by two mechanic (and mountain biker) friends of mine. After all, since they make their livings fixing bikes, and get their kicks by riding them, who could be a better source?

These two suggest the following as an absolute minimum:

tire levers
spare tube and patch kit
air pump
allen wrenches (3, 4, 5, and 6 mm)
six-inch crescent (adjustable-end) wrench
small flat-blade screwdriver
chain rivet tool
spoke wrench

But, while they're on the trail, their personal tool pouches contain these additional items:

channel locks (small)
air gauge
tire valve cap (the metal kind, with a valve-stem remover)
baling wire (ten or so inches, for temporary repairs)
duct tape (small roll for temporary repairs or tire boot)
boot material (small piece of old tire or a large tube patch)

    spare chain link
    rear derailleur pulley
    spare nuts and bolts
    paper towel and tube of waterless hand cleaner

First-aid kit: My personal kit contains the following, sealed inside double Ziploc bags:

    sunscreen
    aspirin
    butterfly-closure bandages
    Band-Aids
    gauze compress pads (a half-dozen 4″ × 4″)
    gauze (1 roll)
    ace bandages or Spenco joint wraps
    Benadryl (an antihistamine, in case of allergic reactions)
    water purification tablets
    Moleskin/Spenco "Second Skin"
    hydrogen peroxide, iodine, or Mercurochrome (some kind of antiseptic)
    snakebite kit

Final Considerations: The authors of this series have done a good job in suggesting that specific items be packed for certain trails—raingear in particular seasons, a hat and gloves for mountain passes, or shades for desert jaunts. Heed their warnings, and think ahead. Good luck.

Dennis Coello
Salt Lake City

NORTHERN CALIFORNIA

Marin

RIDE 1   *MIWOK TO BOBCAT LOOP*

This is a beautiful ten- to twelve-mile loop through the Marin headlands. It can be combined with the Tennessee to Mount Tamalpais loop for a longer ride, or shortened to suit your ability. All of the riding is on wide gravel fire roads, and all of the hills are rideable for the average cyclist.

Scenic rolling hills of grassland and windswept scrub surround you as you ride. The top of this loop reaches one of the highest points in the headlands and has a magnificent view in all directions. Mount Tamalpais lies to the north, the Pacific Ocean to the west, and the Golden Gate Bridge and the city of San Francisco to the south. The lower-lying points of this loop take you to wild, sandy beaches that await your exploration in the Tennessee and Rodeo valleys.

This spectacular land originally was developed by the U.S. Army for coastal defense. Therefore, it escaped commercial development, although an entire city of 20,000 people was planned for Gerbode Valley during the mid-60s. You can enjoy the beauty of the city that never was as you ride through this valley, which lies in the middle of this loop on the Rodeo Beach side.

General location: Just north of the Golden Gate Bridge, in the Golden Gate National Recreation Area.

Elevation change: You can start this loop from two different parking areas. The elevation of the parking area at the firing range is 200′. The Miwok Trail starts at 50′ and reaches its highest elevation at 1,000′. The base of the Marincello Trail is at 100′. The total elevation change for this 10-mile loop is 2,000′.

If you start from the parking area at the north end of the Golden Gate Bridge, where the elevation is 200′, the Coastal Trail climbs to 600′, and the total elevation change for the 11.6-mile loop is 2,800′.

Season: The Marin headlands are beautiful year-round. The winters are mild and wet, with high temperatures usually in the 40s and 50s, often under sunny blue skies. Summer days actually are harder to prepare for, because chilly fog and coastal winds often cover these coastal hills while the inland valleys are simmering in the 90s. Dress in layers to stay comfortable.

Services: Water and rest rooms are available at Rodeo Beach. However, there are no facilities at either parking area, so fill your water bottles before you leave home. For restaurants, groceries, and hotels, Sausalito or San Francisco (across

RIDE 1 *MIWOK TO BOBCAT LOOP*

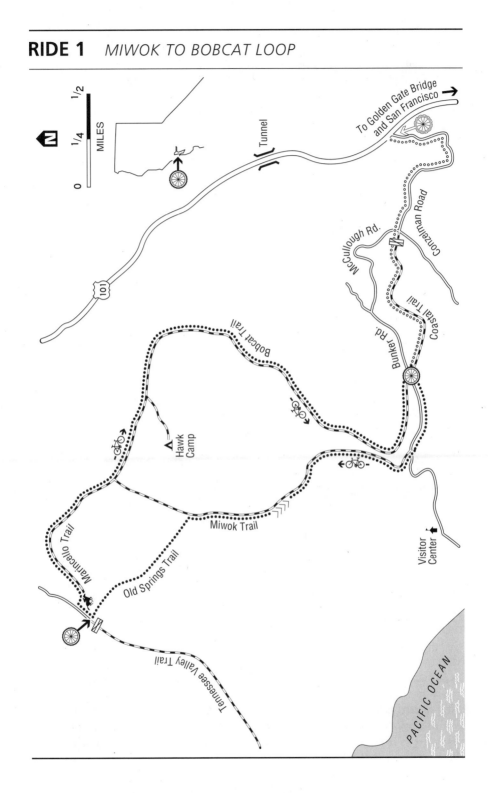

MILES

Tunnel

To Golden Gate Bridge
and San Francisco

Conzelman Road

McCullough Rd.

Coastal Trail

Bunker Rd.

101

Bobcat Trail

Hawk
Camp

Miwok Trail

Martincello Trail

Old Springs Trail

Visitor
Center

Tennessee Valley Trail

PACIFIC OCEAN

the Golden Gate) are your closest choices. If you're interested in camping, you can make reservations for Hawk Camp by calling the Golden Gate National Recreation Area's Fort Cronkite office at (415) 331-1540.

Hazards: Always use caution on descents. These fire roads are usually smooth but ruts can occur from runoff. Remember to yield to pedestrians and horses.

Rescue index: You'll seldom go for very long without seeing another person. If you're alone and need assistance, it's best to try and walk out—you'll probably meet someone on the way.

Land status: Golden Gate National Recreation Area.

Maps:

Golden Gate National Recreation Area, State Parks, and Adjoining Areas, Marin County and San Francisco, CA (published by Erickson Maps, 337 17th Street, Suite 211, Oakland, CA 94612, (510) 893-3685).

A Rambler's Guide to the Trails of Mount Tamalpais and the Marin Headlands (published by Olmstead Bros. Map Co., P.O. Box 5351, Berkeley, CA 94705, (510) 658-4869).

Finding the trail: From San Francisco, take US 101 north across the Golden Gate Bridge and take the first exit after the scenic overlook. Bear left and cross under the freeway; then take the first right towards Fort Barry. This is Conzelman Road. Stay on this road until the intersection with McCullough Road. Turn right down McCullough Road. Bear left onto Bunker Road and park at the first pulloff on your left, which is at the firing range. For the longer ride, take the first left immediately after turning onto Conzelman Road, and park in the large parking area on the left. Ride to the intersection with McCullough Road to pick up the Coastal Trail.

Sources of additional information:

Noe Valley Cyclery
4193 24th Street
San Francisco, CA 94114
(415) 647-0886

Notes on the trail: If you park at the north end of the Golden Gate Bridge, it's just under a mile and a half of paved uphill to the intersection of Conzelman and McCullough Road. Ride around the gate and onto the fire road, which is between the two paved roads. This is the Coastal Trail; it ends at the firing range, where the shorter ride begins.

To pick up the shorter loop, turn left onto Bunker Road towards the ocean and Fort Cronkite. Immediately after crossing a bridge with a pond on your right and Rodeo Lagoon on the left, take a hard right past a gate onto the Miwok Trail, a fire road. Stay left on the Miwok Trail when the Bobcat Trail forks right. Just before the Miwok Trail begins climbing sharply towards the white Federal Aviation Administration (FAA) directional tower, go left on Old Springs Trail, which drops down into Tennessee Valley. The trail takes you to the back of the

The Bobcat Trail is in the headlands of Mount Tamalpais.

stables. Walk or ride your bike through the stables and turn right at the next fire road, which is Marincello. If you need a portable toilet, there is one located here at the Tennessee Valley parking lot. The Marincello Trail climbs back up the ridge, where it ends. Continue straight onto the Bobcat Trail.

Just a third of a mile from this junction, a trail on the right leaves for Hawk Camp, which is a primitive camp just a half mile off of the Bobcat Trail. It's a beautiful spot to watch hawks, and also overlooks the site of a once-proposed city of 20,000. There is no water at Hawk Camp, but there is a portable toilet.

Back on Bobcat, continue on down the hill and stay to the right at every intersection. This route will loop you back around Gerbode Valley into Rodeo Valley and to the start of the Miwok Trail. If you started from the Golden Gate Bridge, continue past the firing range and return the way you came.

RIDE 2 *TENNESSEE VALLEY TO MOUNT TAMALPAIS*

This is a very scenic 20-mile loop up and down Mount Tamalpais, known locally as Mount Tam. From Tennessee Valley to the top of Mount Tamalpais, there are two hills. A fire road called the Coastal Trail climbs 500' to the top of the ridge. The descent to Muir Beach is the steepest part of the whole ride, so keep your weight back and take it slow. At Muir Beach, dirt turns to pavement for a short distance on CA 1 and Muir Woods Road. The Deer Park fire road begins the second and longest hill; it's steeper than the Coastal Trail but beautiful as it ascends through Muir Woods, an old-growth redwood forest. At the Pantoll Ranger Station there are rest rooms and water for refilling your bottles before you attack the last short climb to the West Point Inn on Mount Tamalpais. You'll ride up the Old Stage Road and down the Old Railroad Grade, both of them smooth roads with gentle inclines. On the descent, do not exceed 15 miles per hour—this speed limit is strictly enforced. The Old Railroad Grade brings you down into the town of Mill Valley; from here to Tennessee Valley, you ride pavement.

The fire roads are all one-lane gravel and dirt roads, while the rest of the ride is on pavement. You begin your ride through the Marin headlands in open grassland with breathtaking views of the ocean. At the top of the ridge, look south to see San Francisco glistening through the hills. Drop down onto Muir Beach and the ocean is yours. The scenery changes to ancient redwoods as you climb through Muir Woods. From the West Point Inn, the view of San Francisco is again marvelous.

Riding is great throughout these scenically diverse public lands, which are comprised of the Marin Municipal Water District, the Golden Gate National Recreation Area, and Mount Tamalpais State Park. It's wonderful and rare to have so wild an area so close to a major population center as San Francisco.

On this ride, there are many beautiful spots. My favorites are the climb through Muir Woods, the view from the West Point Inn (all the more enjoyable because you know it's the summit of your ride), and the smooth downhill of the Railroad Grade. The railroad ran for over thirty years, beginning in 1896, and carried people up to the platform at the Double Bow Knot or on up to the West Point Inn. From the Inn, people could hike to the summit of Mount Tam or take a stage coach down Old Stage Road to the coastal town of Bolinas.

Besides its historical flavor, this loop offers chances to spot birds at every turn. The most common bird that you may sight is the turkey vulture, but there are many more that share this landscape. Along the coast, you'll see brown pelicans, gulls, cormorants, and terns. The headlands also lie along a principal flyway for hawks and other raptors, and in the prime months of August and September, hundreds may be seen in an afternoon. For more information contact the Golden Gate Raptor Observatory at (415) 331-0730.

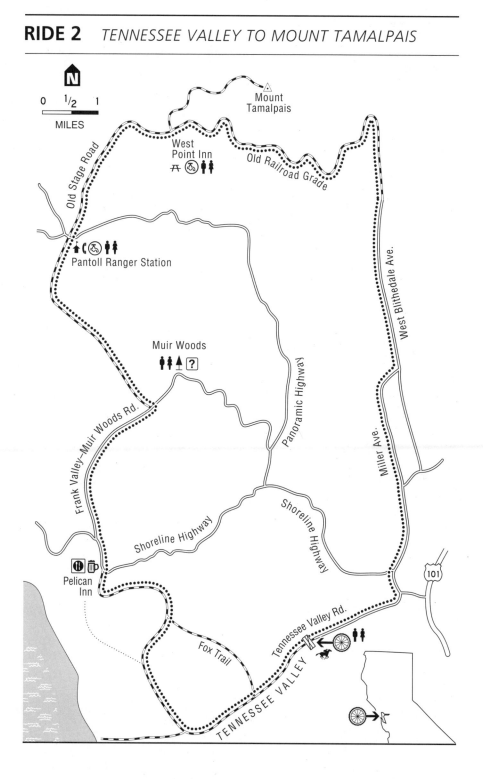

General location: Two miles north of Sausalito, to the west of CA 1, the Pacific Coast Highway.

Elevation change: This loop begins at 50' in the Tennessee Valley parking area and climbs to 500' at the top of the Coastal Trail. You drop down to sea level at Muir Beach. The summit of the ride measures 1,800' at the West Point Inn. Total elevation gain is 2,250'.

Season: You'll enjoy riding the Marin headlands and Mount Tamalpais year-round. Winter is the rainy season but there are many clear days and temperatures are mild, usually in the 40s and 50s. Summer is the dry season, but, ironically, coastal fog often blankets the area despite inland temperatures in the 90s (often within just an hour's riding distance on the bike). Your best bet for staying comfortable is to dress in layers. September tends to be the clearest, warmest month, with coastal temperatures in the 70s.

Services: Water, rest rooms, and telephones are available at Muir Beach, Pantoll Ranger Station, and the West Point Inn. In the town of Mill Valley, there are restaurants, grocery stores, and hotels.

Hazards: This entire loop lies within a very popular recreation area, so watch out for other people hiking, cycling, and horseback riding, and observe good mountain bike etiquette as described in the Afterword at the back of this book. Because many horses are spooked by bicycles, always ask equestrians whether you should dismount and walk your bike around them. Hikers also appreciate riders slowing down or stopping when passing.

From Mill Valley, be careful riding in traffic back to the Tennessee Valley parking area.

Rescue index: You're not far from help at any point on this well-traveled ride. Pay phone locations are listed under services.

Land status: Marin Municipal Water District, Golden Gate National Recreation Area, and Mount Tamalpais State Park.

Maps:

Golden Gate National Recreation Area, State Parks, and Adjoining Areas, Marin County and San Francisco, CA (published by Erickson Maps, 337 17th Street, Suite 211, Oakland, CA 94612, (510) 893-3685).

A Rambler's Guide to the Trails of Mount Tamalpais and the Marin Headlands (published by Olmstead Bros. Map Co., P.O. Box 5351, Berkeley, CA 94705, (510) 658-4869).

Finding the trail: From San Francisco, take US 101 north to the Stinson Beach/CA 1 exit. Within a mile, you'll see a sign for Tennessee Valley Road. Take this left turn and follow Tennessee Valley Road to the end, where there is a large parking area.

Sources of additional information:

Noe Valley Cyclery
4193 24th Street

From many areas in the Mount Tamalpais headlands you can see San Francisco.

San Francisco, CA 94114
(415) 647-0886

Superintendent, Golden Gate National Recreation Area
National Park Service
Building 201, Fort Mason
San Francisco, CA 94123
(415) 556-2920

Green Pedalers
(415) 334-6908

Notes on the trail: From the parking area to Tennessee Valley Road, ride around the gate and down the valley. One mile down the valley, the pavement turns to dirt. After passing the ranger's house farther along the dirt road, the Coastal Trail, a fire road rises to the right out of the valley. A small sign will direct you to Muir Beach.

Upon reaching the false summit, be careful to avoid the Coastal Trail down to Pirates Cove. Stay on the fire road as it winds away from the coast to the intersection with the Fox Trail. Turn left onto the Fox Trail. It's only a little farther to the top of the ridge, where the Fox Trail meets the Coyote Ridge Trail. Head down to the left to reach Muir Beach.

Explore the beach if you like, and refill your bottle at the faucet hidden in the tree stump. Exit out the parking lot to the intersection with CA 1.

The Pelican Inn on your left is an authentic English pub (closed Mondays). Take CA 1 north briefly as it veers left; turn right toward Muir Woods National Monument, up the Frank Valley–Muir Woods Road. Ride on the pavement up the valley along Redwood Creek for 2 miles. Take a left on the Deer Park fire road. If you reach the Muir Woods National Monument parking lot, you've gone too far.

After you climb up through the redwoods, turn right at the T-intersection and continue straight ahead to the Pantoll Ranger Station. This is another good spot to refill water bottles. Exit the Pantoll Ranger Station on the pavement. Cross Panoramic Drive and head right onto the dirt Old Stage Road before winding along Mount Tamalpais to the West Point Inn. This is the place to take in a spectacular view before dropping down into Mill Valley. (If you'd like to go to the summit of Mount Tamalpais from here, it's just a short detour. Take the fire road that curves around the left-hand side of the Inn. Follow this fire road up until it meets a paved road, where you'll turn right and continue until you reach the turnaround atop the East Peak. When you're done admiring the view, return the way you came.)

Take the Old Railroad Grade, a fire road on the right-hand side of the West Point Inn. Note the two 15-mph speed limit signs—they are serious. As you head down, there are two forks. The first fork has a fire road to the left, the Hoo Koo E Koo Trail. Stay to the right here. Farther down the trail is the old railroad platform, and just beyond this is the second fork, where you should go left instead of going straight. Your fire road ends about halfway down the mountain at a barrier; go around it to get on the pavement. Ride on the pavement for less than a mile; where the pavement takes a hairpin curve to the right, you turn left onto another dirt fire road. This goes down to West Blithedale Avenue.

At the end of the fire road, lift your bike over the gate, turn left onto the pavement, and ride on into Mill Valley. Turn right onto Throckmorton, where West Blithedale becomes East Blithedale. Follow Throckmorton for one block and turn left onto Miller Avenue. Take Miller Avenue past Mount Tam High School and watch for bike route signs that will direct you to cross over Miller Avenue and get on a bike path. Once on the bike path, you'll ride about a half mile and cross two bridges. Immediately after the second bridge, turn right. Follow the bike path to another, third bridge. Cut to the right and ride or walk under the bridge (this section can be wet at high tide). Follow the trail along the creek until it rejoins Tennessee Valley Road. Continue on up the paved road to the parking area.

RIDE 3   *ELDRIDGE GRADE TO MOUNT TAMALPAIS*

This is a 17.5-mile loop that climbs Mount Tamalpais from the north side. It has some long climbs and some great downhills. You'll ride mostly on well-maintained fire roads with short stretches on pavement. The most difficult section is the top of Eldridge Grade, where the steep and rough trail makes you wonder who talked you into this ride. Once you hit the pavement, there's just a little more climbing to the top of the East Peak. Dropping back down on the Lagunitas–Rock Springs fire road is steep and rough in some spots—just take it slowly.

The scenery on this loop is beautiful. Beginning at Phoenix Lake, the trails run through hardwood forests of oak, bay, buckeye, and madrone. This section is especially pleasant on hot summer days because the forest cover keeps the trails shaded. Above Lake Lagunitas on the Eldridge Grade, the large trees give way to low scrub brush as you climb toward the summit. From the East Peak, there's an impressive view of San Francisco and the ocean.

Lake Lagunitas is one of the prettiest spots on the whole mountain. On the trail around the lake there are several fun water crossings that you may either splash through or traverse on small bridges. The lake attracts many sea birds such as gulls, coots, plovers, and cormorants. If you choose to ride all the way to the top, it's always a thrill to look down from the East Peak and congratulate yourself for having made it up there.

General location: About 9 miles north of the Golden Gate Bridge on US 101 and 3 miles west on Sir Francis Drake Boulevard.
Elevation change: The ride begins at Phoenix Lake, elevation 180', and climbs to 783' at Lake Lagunitas. The top of Eldridge Grade is at 2,200' and East Peak reaches 2,571'. Total elevation change is 2,391'.
Season: Like the other coastal rides in this area, this one is worthwhile in any month of the year. You'll find sunny days year-round, with usual highs in the 40s and 50s in winter and in the 70s in summer. Be prepared for rain during the temperate winter months and for coastal fog during the summer.
Services: There are rest rooms and a phone at the parking lot by Bon Tempe

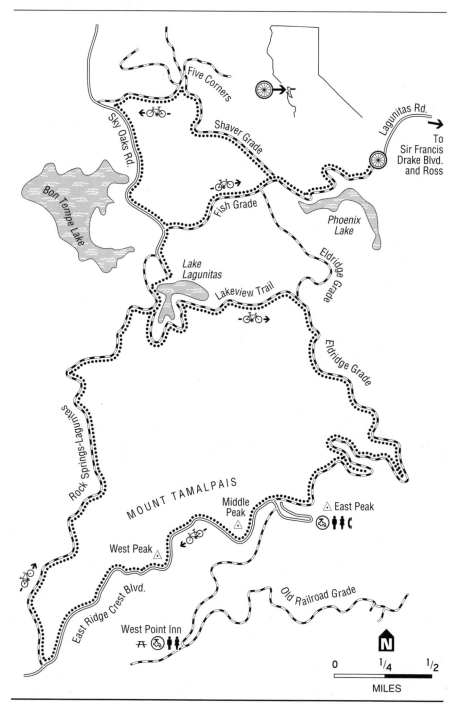

Five Corners

Sky Oaks Rd.

Shaver Grade

Lagunitas Rd.

To
Sir Francis
Drake Blvd.
and Ross

Bon Tempe Lake

Fish Grade

Phoenix
Lake

Lake
Lagunitas

Lakeview Trail

Eldridge Grade

Eldridge Grade

Rock Springs-Lagunitas

MOUNT TAMALPAIS

Middle
Peak

East Peak

West Peak

West Point Inn

East Ridge Crest Blvd.

Old Railroad Grade

N

0   1/4   1/2

MILES

Lake. Other services are located on Sir Francis Drake Boulevard, where you'll find hotels, restaurants, and grocery stores.

Hazards: Some of the downhill sections on this ride are steep, so keep your machine under control. As always, be on the lookout for other people using the trails.

Rescue index: You're not far from help at any point on this well-traveled ride. Pay phone locations are listed under services.

Land Status: Mount Tamalpais State Park and the Marin Municipal Water District.

Maps:

Golden Gate National Recreation Area, State Parks, and Adjoining Areas, Marin County and San Francisco, CA (published by Erickson Maps, 337 17th Street, Suite 211, Oakland, CA 94612, (510) 893-3685).

A Rambler's Guide to the Trails of Mount Tamalpais and the Marin Headlands (published by Olmstead Bros. Map Co., P.O. Box 5351, Berkeley, CA 94705, (510) 658-4869).

Finding the trail: From the Golden Gate Bridge, take US 101 north for 9 miles. Take the exit for San Anselmo and Sir Francis Drake Boulevard. Follow Sir Francis Drake west for about 3 miles. Past the College of Marin, take a left onto Lagunitas Road. Follow Lagunitas all the way until it dead-ends into the parking lot at Phoenix Lake, where you'll start your ride.

Sources of additional Information:

Noe Valley Cyclery
4193 24th Street
San Francisco, CA 94114
(415) 647-0886

Notes on the trail: Take the fire road up from the Phoenix Lake parking area to the intersection with Shaver Grade, Fish Grade, and Eldridge Grade. Turn right onto Shaver Grade. At Five Corners, go left to stay on Shaver Grade. At the top of the hill, you'll intersect with Sky Oaks Road, which is paved. Turn left here and ride clockwise around Bon Tempe Lake. The paved road dead-ends at a parking lot, where there are rest rooms and a phone on the left.

Continuing straight past these facilities and another fire road that leaves to the left, you'll reach the spillway of Lake Lagunitas. Turn right across the spillway and ride counterclockwise around the lake. You'll see one trail entering on the right; this is the Lagunitas–Rock Springs fire road, on which you'll return to the lake if you do the whole loop. On the far side of the lake, at the T-intersection, turn right onto the unsigned Lakeview Trail, which will bring you up to Eldridge Grade.

Here, you have the option of shortening your ride. Going left on Eldridge will take you back down to Phoenix Lake. (There are two intersections on the way down: go left at the first one and right at the second.) Going right on Eldridge

Grand oaks, which provide cooling shade on hot summer days, line the beginning of the Eldridge Grade.

will take you up to the top of Mount Tam. The East Peak vista point is just up to the left.

After taking time out to enjoy the stunning view, head right, down East Ridgecrest, and ride the pavement to the Lagunitas–Rock Springs fire road. Be careful not to miss the trailhead, which sometimes is hard to see from this direction. Watch for the gate and take the dirt fire road going off to the right. After a short climb, you'll make a wild 3-mile descent back to Lake Lagunitas. Turn left at the lake, and in a short distance you will be back at the spillway. Go back across the spillway, through the parking lot, onto Sky Oaks Road; then take the first right down Fish Grade. This is a steep hill, so use extra caution. Continue straight at the next intersection, which will take you back to Phoenix Lake. Ride alongside the lake back to the parking lot.

East Bay

RIDE 4   *TILDEN PARK, NIMITZ WAY, AND WILDCAT CREEK LOOP*

This mellow eight-mile loop ride (or nine-and-a-half-mile out-and-back) features some excellent views of the San Francisco Bay. The easy out-and-back begins along the Nimitz Way, a paved bike path that follows the rolling hills of the San Pablo Ridge. The surrounding grassy hillsides are still leased for grazing, as occasional gates can attest. To the east are views of San Pablo Dam and the Sobrante Ridge, while Berkeley and San Francisco Bay lie to the west. If you continue on the loop there's a great downhill, then mostly level riding along Wildcat Creek. It's not until the last mile that you get the chance to do some hill climbing. Dropping down the ridge on gravel fire roads, you ride through groves of eucalyptus. Wildcat Canyon features scattered oaks and willows, as well as a variety of flowers along the creek.

The Tilden Nature Area attracts many birds. Look for mallards on Jewell Lake and for towhees, jays, juncos, robins, and sparrows in the trees.

General location: In the hills just east of Berkeley.
Elevation change: The ride begins at 1,040′ and drops to 400′, returning to 1,040′ for a total elevation gain of 640′.
Season: This area is best ridden in the drier months of April through September to avoid mud during the rainy season.
Services: All services are available in Berkeley.
Hazards: After it rains, these trails turn into the worst muck you've ever seen. It sticks to your tires, clogs up your brakes, and is no fun to ride in. Give this area (and everything north of Inspiration Point) a few days to dry out after a rain.

In sunny weather, weekend traffic can be heavy in Tilden Park. Please remember to slow down and warn people that you are behind them when passing. Little children are especially unpredictable, so pass them at a snail's pace.
Rescue index: In this very busy park, if you need assistance, someone will always come along. A phone is located partway through this ride at Jewel Lake in the nature study area.
Land status: Tilden Regional Park and Wildcat Regional Park. Part of the East Bay Regional Park District, created from water company land in 1934 by a vote of area citizens.
Maps: A free pamphlet is (sometimes) available at the beginning of this ride, but it only shows Tilden Park and none of Wildcat Canyon. For a more com-

RIDE 4 *TILDEN PARK, NIMITZ WAY, AND WILDCAT CREEK LOOP*

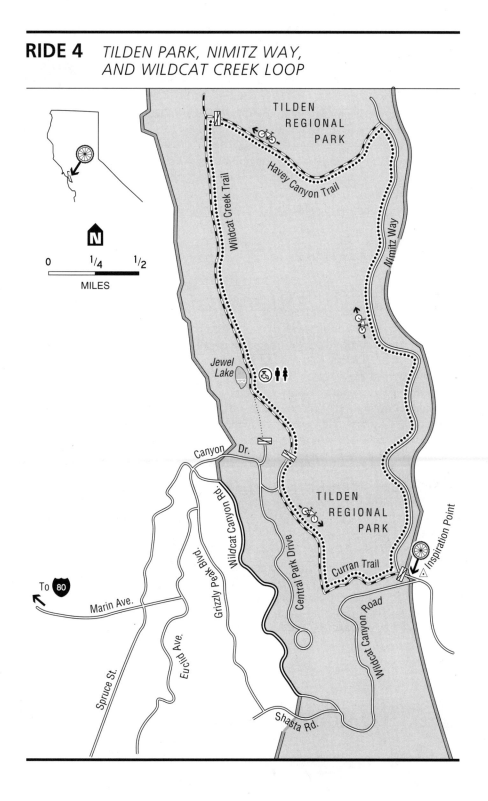

TILDEN REGIONAL PARK

Havey Canyon Trail

Wildcat Creek Trail

Nimitz Way

N

0   1/4   1/2
MILES

Jewel Lake

Canyon   Dr.

Wildcat Canyon Rd.

Grizzly Peak Blvd.

To 80

Marin Ave.

Euclid Ave.

Spruce St.

Central Park Drive

TILDEN REGIONAL PARK

Curran Trail

Inspiration Point

Wildcat Canyon Road

Shasta Rd.

prehensive map of this area, see *Trails of the East Bay Hills: Tilden, Wildcat Canyon, and Briones Park*. Published by Olmstead Bros. Map Co., P.O. Box 5351, Berkeley, CA 94704, (510) 658-4869.

Finding the trail: From San Francisco, take Interstate 80 east over the Bay Bridge to CA 24. Take the Fish Ranch Road exit just past the Caldicott Tunnel. (Stay in the right lane going through the tunnel.) In 1 mile, turn right at the stop sign onto Grizzly Peak Road and continue on this for 3 miles. At the next stop sign, turn right onto Shasta Road. In a half mile, there's another stop sign. Continue straight to merge with Wildcat Canyon Road. Follow signs for Inspiration Point, approximately 1 mile ahead, and park your car there.

Sources of additional information:

East Bay Regional Park District
11500 Skyline Boulevard
Oakland, CA 94619
(510) 531-9300

Notes on the trail: The views from the Nimitz Way bike path are beautiful. It's a thrill to be in the middle of this wild country and look out over the rooftops of the Bay area. All the East Bay regional parks have this quality of feeling a million miles away from the tensions of the city.

After the paved Nimitz Way ends in 4 miles, there are many options. You may continue on down one of several trails, or do the following loop. Double back and take the first fire road to the right. This is the Havey Canyon Trail, a smooth dirt road that descends into Wildcat Canyon. Since this trail is shaded, it can take several days to dry out after a rain, so give it a few days or you'll find yourself in a mud trap. Be sure to close the two gates you'll pass through on this trail. After the second gate, turn left onto the Wildcat Creek Trail, which will take you back into Tilden through the nature study area. At Jewell Lake there are flush toilets, water, and a phone. There's only one way for bikes to ride through the nature area and it's well signed.

The trail returns to pavement after a fire gate. Follow the road to the right, then turn left at the Lone Oak picnic area, onto the dirt Wildcat Gorge Trail. A sign here notifies you that this trail is closed in wet weather. (If the trail is wet, continue straight on the pavement and turn left onto Wildcat Canyon Road; follow it back up to Inspiration Point.) Ride the Wildcat Gorge Trail along the creek until you see a spillway on the right. The trail then takes a hard left and becomes the Curran Trail, which climbs uphill and returns to the parking area at Inspiration Point.

RIDE 5 *REDWOOD PARK / WEST TO EAST RIDGE*

Redwood Park is a beautiful two-thousand-acre park, through which the eight-mile ride travels over two ridges before dropping down into a valley at the south end. Riding along the West Ridge, you can see Oakland to the west and heavily forested Redwood Canyon to the east; from the East Ridge, you can see San Leandro Reservoir. This area was heavily logged in the 1850s but second- and sometimes third-growth redwood trees have reached imposing size. Local historians believe that the remains of one tree in this park indicate a diameter of 33.5 feet when it was alive. Although nothing of this size still grows in the park, the young redwoods are impressive nevertheless.

During most of this ride, you'll need to focus on the trail, which consists of dirt and gravel fire roads. Portions of both the East and the West Ridge become rough from runoff, and on the steep downhill sections you'll need to go slow enough to maneuver around the ruts. These stretches can be a little scary for some riders with little experience on descents. The steep uphill climb at the beginning of the East Ridge Trail can be just as daunting, but there is no law against dismounting and taking a short walk uphill while on a leisurely ride.

Once on top of the ridge, the trail becomes gentle and rolling. At the south entrance, take the time to ride up the Stream Trail to the old church site before continuing up to the East Ridge. Only the concrete foundation of the old church remains, but this detour is a short, level, and lovely ride along Redwood Creek.

General location: In the hills just east of Oakland.
Elevation change: Skyline Gate is at 1,280'; from there, it is a gentle climb to the archery center at 1,400'. The trail drops down to 560' at the beginning of the East Ridge Trail. In a short distance you climb to 900', and then more gradually to 1,300' just before Skyline Gate. Total elevation change is 860'.
Season: Redwood Park is rideable year-round.
Services: Water, rest rooms, and a pay phone can be found at the Skyline Gate parking area. The park office at the southern end of this ride also has a pay phone. All services are available in Oakland.
Hazards: The steep descents can be difficult and although many riders will not worry about the last section of the West Ridge Trail, some may choose to walk. Stay to the right and keep your speed under control on the way down.
Rescue index: You can get help at the park office at the southern end of this route.
Land status: Redwood Regional Park, East Bay Regional Park District.
Maps: Free maps of Redwood Park are available at several of the park's entrances. For a larger map showing Redwood Park and contiguous parks in the area, see *A Rambler's Guide to the Trails of the East Bay Hills: Redwood,*

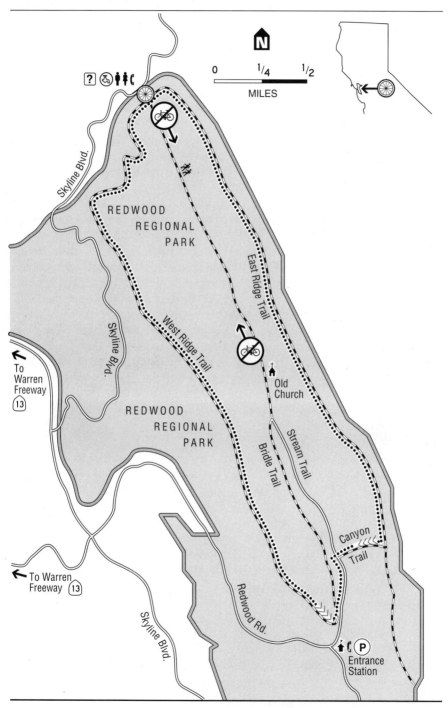

Chabot, Las Trampas, Sibley, and Joaquin Miller Parks, published by Olmsted Bros. Map Co., P.O. Box 5351, Berkeley, CA 94705, (510) 658-4869.

Finding the trail: From San Francisco, take I-80 east over the Bay Bridge to CA 24. Take CA 13 south to Joaquin Miller Road and go east. At the top of the hill, turn left onto Skyline Boulevard. Follow this road beyond the archery center and Carisbrook Drive, then turn right into the Skyline Gate parking area to start your ride.

Sources of additional information:

East Bay Regional Park District
11500 Skyline Boulevard
Oakland, CA 94619
(510) 531-9300

RIDE 6 *LAKE CHABOT*

This fun nine-and-a-half-mile loop has two moderate hills, some sporty downhills, and lots of level riding. All the trails open to mountain bikers are dirt and gravel fire roads. The first part of the ride traverses hillsides of open grassland and scrub. Once on the Brandon Trail, you'll wind through eucalyptus forest and occasional meadows. Along the Goldenrod Trail and the west shore of Lake Chabot, look for willows, elderberry, and bigleaf maple. The easy ride along the lakeshore offers entertaining glimpses of the ducks, grebes, and coots that inhabit the lake.

Lake Chabot, the dominant feature of Anthony Chabot Regional Park, is manmade. In 1875, an engineer by the name of Anthony Chabot borrowed techniques used for gold mining and washed tons of dirt off the surrounding hillsides into San Leandro Creek to form a dam. Chinese laborers spread the dirt and then 200 wild horses were driven back and forth to pack it down. Lake Chabot now serves as a reservoir for emergency use only. Its shoreline remains relatively stable and lush. People often go out on the lake for rainbow trout; largemouth bass; bluegill; black crappie; red-ear and green sunfish; channel, white, and brown bullhead catfish; and carp.

General location: Just east of San Leandro.
Elevation change: The elevation of the parking area is 300'. The first hill climbs to 520' and then drops down to 240' at the Willow Park Golf Course. The second hill rises to 800' and takes a long, gentle drop to the stone bridge at 520'. From the bridge, the road climbs up to 620' before dropping down along the lakeshore at 300', for a total elevation change of 580'.
Season: These trails are fun to ride throughout the year.

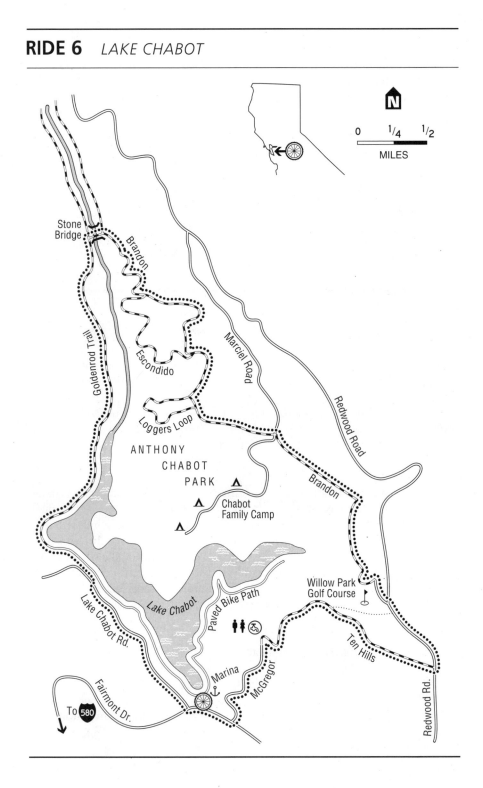

N

0   1/4   1/2
MILES

Stone
Bridge

Brandon

Escondido

Marciel Road

Goldenrod Trail

Loggers Loop

Redwood Road

ANTHONY
CHABOT
PARK

Chabot
Family Camp

Brandon

Willow Park
Golf Course

Lake Chabot

Paved Bike Path

Lake Chabot Rd.

Ten Hills

Marina

McGregor

Redwood Rd.

To 580

Fairmont Dr.

Services: You'll find water and rest rooms at the top of the first hill. There are phones at the Willow Park Golf Course and at Chabot Family Camp, a public campground in the park that is open year-round on a first-come, first-served basis. No reservations are taken. The campground has good hot showers! For restaurants and groceries, go back across I-580 and into San Leandro.

Hazards: As always, please be careful when crossing and riding paved stretches, such as the short section of Redwood Road, and remember to yield to pedestrians and horses.

Rescue index: This is a very busy park, so if you need assistance, others should be along soon.

Land status: Anthony Chabot Regional Park, East Bay Regional Park District.

Maps:

A *Rambler's Guide to the Trails of the East Bay Hills: Redwood, Chabot, Las Trampas, Sibley, and Joaquin Miller Parks* (published by Olmsted Bros. Map Co., P.O. Box 5351, Berkeley, CA 94705, (510) 658-4869).

Finding the trail: From San Francisco, take I-80 east over the Bay Bridge to I-580 south. Take the Fairmont Drive exit and turn left. Follow Fairmont up and over the hill. At the bottom of the hill, Lake Chabot is on the left. Park your car on the right side of the road across from the lake.

Sources of additional information:

East Bay Regional Park District
11500 Skyline Boulevard
Oakland, CA 94619
(510) 531-9300

Notes on the trail: From the parking area, ride down the road and turn left onto McGregor, which is a dead-end access road to a park building. Turn right just past this building onto the Ten Hills fire road. Follow that until the T-intersection and turn left onto Redwood Road. At the bottom of the paved downhill, turn left into the Willow Park Golf Course. Follow the driveway back into the right corner of the parking area and pick up the Brandon Trail. At the top of the hill, cross the paved road and continue on Brandon all the way to the stone bridge. Cross the bridge and turn left (south) on the Goldenrod Trail. This becomes a paved path along the west shore of the lake and takes you back to the parking area.

San Jose

RIDE 7   GRANT RANCH COUNTY PARK

Grant Ranch County Park has some beautiful riding but is hilly and can get very hot in the summer. Two loops are suggested—2.5 or 9.6 miles long—but many combinations are possible. The trails open to mountain bikes in this park are wide fire roads, mostly dirt with some gravel. Certain areas can get very muddy so trails are closed for 48 hours after a heavy rain. The longer loop has several tough hills. On the first hill, the dirt is loose and the trail is rutted. The next rough section is on the Digger Pine Trail, which becomes quite rocky with a number of short but steep ascents. All longer rides in this park are hilly and trail conditions vary from year to year.

Grant Ranch County Park is located in the Hamilton Mountains just below the Lick Observatory. If you're curious about astronomy, ride or drive up to the observatory for a free tour. If you enjoy bird-watching, check out the reservoir, which attracts many birds including kestrels, kingfishers, killdeer, wood ducks, juncos, and hawks. For a complete bird list, stop at the Visitor Center.

General location: Just south of San Jose.
Elevation change: Parking is at 1,600' and the trail drops down to 1,400' at Circle Corral. From here, the trail climbs to 2,080' at Eagle Lake. After a short descent, the trail gains its summit at 2,600' before dropping back down to 1,600'. Total elevation change for the longer loop is 1,280'. The shorter, 2.5-mile option only changes by a total of approximately 200'.
Season: Grant Ranch has mild winters and hot summers. Rainy weather in the winter usually makes the trails too muddy to ride, but as drier spring weather arrives, the hillsides are lush, green, and dotted with California poppy (the state flower) and wild mustard. When summer arrives, the hills turn golden brown and the temperatures rise. Carry plenty of water and ride early in the day. Fall brings the beauty of the oak leaves changing, and cooler temperatures that make riding more comfortable.
Services: Water and rest rooms are available at the trailhead. For grocery stores, restaurants, and hotels, return to Tully Road and US 101.
Hazards: Remember to yield to both horses and hikers. Slow down around blind curves because someone might be coming the other way.
Rescue index: Mountain bikers are required to wear a helmet when riding in this park. Trails are patroled by rangers on mountain bikes and they'll give you

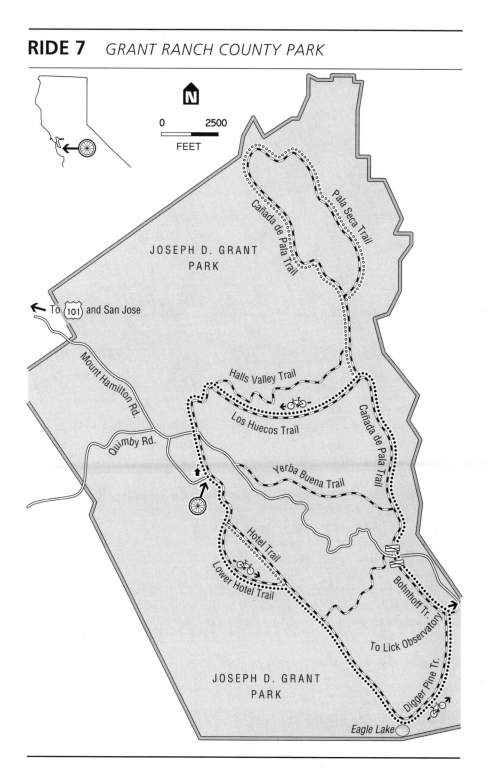

N

0   2500
FEET

JOSEPH D. GRANT
PARK

Pala Seca Trail

Cañada de Pala Trail

To (101) and San Jose

Mount Hamilton Rd.

Halls Valley Trail

Quimby Rd.

Los Huecos Trail

Cañada de Pala Trail

Yerba Buena Trail

Hotel Trail

Lower Hotel Trail

Bohnhoff Tr.

To Lick Observatory

Digger Pine Tr.

JOSEPH D. GRANT
PARK

Eagle Lake

Start your ride at the Grant Ranch County Park at the Visitor Center parking lot. Remember to close the gates.

a ticket for not protecting your head. If you need help on the trail, return to the Visitor Center for assistance.

Land status: Santa Clara County parkland.

Maps: There is an excellent free map available at the Visitor Center. Trails and mileage are marked.

Finding the trail: Just south of where I-280 and I-880 merge into US 101, take the Tully Road exit heading east. Turn right on Quimby and follow it as it becomes a small two-lane road. Quimby climbs up and over a steep hill and intersects with Mount Hamilton Road in approximately 4 miles. Turn right, and right again into the park. There's a $3 day-use fee. Park near the Hotel Trail and Visitor Center.

Sources of additional information:

J. D. Grant County Park
18405 Mount Hamilton Road
San Jose, CA 95140
(408) 274-6121

Notes on the trail: Beginning at the Visitor Center, go through the two livestock gates to the start of the Hotel Trail. After .2 miles, veer right onto the Lower Hotel Trail at the Circle Corral. For the shorter loop, turn left and return to the Visitor Center. To continue on the longer loop, turn right into the trees, where the trail immediately begins to climb. In 1.75 miles is Eagle Lake, 680' higher than Circle Corral. Take a break at this very pretty spot.

You'll resume the longer ride by heading left at Eagle Lake. A quick descent takes you down into a canyon where the Digger Pine Trail follows the stream. One mile past Eagle Lake, turn left onto the Bohnhoff Trail and start another steep climb. The trail levels off along the ridge before a quick descent to Mount Hamilton Road. There are gates on either side of the road; please shut the gates after passing through them. After another climb you'll be rewarded with a superb 360-degree view.

You can add an extra 2 miles by doing the Cãnada de Pala to the Pala Seca Trail and looping back to the Los Huecos Trail. However, if you're ready to call it a day, continue onto the Los Huecos Trail, and turn left there for a descent to the reservoir. This is a great spot for bird-watching. At Mount Hamilton Road, turn left, and very soon turn right through a gate to return to the parking area.

RIDE 8   *HENRY COE STATE PARK*

In general, Henry Coe State Park is a very challenging area for mountain biking because it is so hilly. However, this five-mile out-and-back ride is an easy one, suitable for the intermediate mountain biker. There's a short, moderate incline at the beginning of the ride, but the rest is downhill through rolling terrain into Manzanita Point Group Camp. The trail is well signed and follows a wide fire road of gravel and dirt.

Henry Coe is California's second-largest state park at 67,000 acres. Elevations range from 800' to 3,500', resulting in diverse scenery that includes grassland, oak and ponderosa pine forests, and deep canyons. A variety of animals call this park home. There's a good chance you'll see deer, and watch for raccoon, skunk, fox, and bobcat at dusk. Wild turkeys and wild pigs that have been introduced from outside the park live here as well. Birds are numerous and include the golden eagle.

For most riders, this brief out-and-back will be a nice afternoon ride, and a good introduction to the variety of mountain biking in this area. In certain parts of the park, additional trails are open to mountain bikers. These trails are farther away from park headquarters and are suitable for the intermediate to advanced rider. Give yourself the better part of a whole day to explore these longer trails, which take longer to ride than you might think in this hilly country.

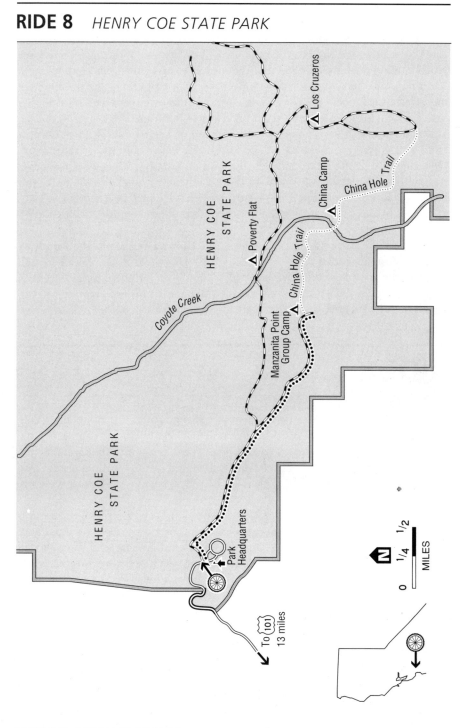

Henry Coe State Park features well-marked trails.

General location: South of San Jose and 13 miles east of US 101 in Morgan Hill.
Elevation change: Your starting point in the parking area is at 2,600′. The trail climbs 800′ before dropping down to 2,150′. There's a short climb of 50′ up to Manzanita Point, the outer end of this out-and-back.
Season: The best riding is in the spring, when the hills still are green but the trails are not too wet, and in the fall, when the oak leaves turn colors and the temperatures reach the comfortable 60s and 70s. Summer can be scorchingly hot (carry extra water), and winter rains sometimes close the trails altogether.
Services: Rest rooms, water, a pay phone, and camping facilities are available at the parking area next to park headquarters. There are also several wilderness campsites available to bikers; call park headquarters for more information. For all other services, go to Morgan Hill.
Hazards: Watch out for other trail users and always yield to horses and hikers.

Rattlesnakes are found in the park. They are not aggressive but will defend themselves if harassed. If you see one, leave it alone!

Ticks are also found in this area, so check your skin and clothing carefully at the end of the ride and get rid of these pests before they dig in.
Rescue index: In any emergency, return to park headquarters for assistance. There is a pay phone located there.

Land status: California state park.

Maps: Park headquarters supplies a small, free map that shows what areas are open to mountain bikes and also indicates mileages to many points in the park. The museum shop has larger, more comprehensive maps for sale.

Finding the trail: From US 101, take the East Dunne Avenue exit and bear east at Morgan Hill. Follow the signs up a narrow, winding road for 13 miles past Anderson Reservoir until you reach the dead end at park headquarters. There's a $3 day-use parking fee for the small lot in which you'll park your car.

Sources of additional information:

Henry W. Coe State Park
P.O. Box 846
Morgan Hill, CA 95038
(408) 779-2728

Santa Cruz

RIDE 9   *APTOS CREEK FIRE ROAD / NISENE MARKS STATE PARK*

This 18-mile out-and-back ride is located just south of Santa Cruz and east of Aptos in the Forest of Nisene Marks State Park. The trail avoids cars and stays in the park on an old logging road that climbs gradually.

Your destination on this ride is Sand Point Overlook, which affords the best view in the entire park. Looking south, you see Monterey Bay. To the southwest is the town of Santa Cruz. To the west is Ben Lomond Ridge, and to the northwest, the Santa Cruz Mountains. From Sand Point Overlook, it's a lively downhill ride back to the town of Aptos.

Most of the trail runs through second-growth redwood forest. The area once was dominated by majestic redwoods but was thoroughly logged in the early 1900s, leaving only huge stumps that can be seen on both sides of the old road. The forest is now a blend of bigleaf maple, red alder, Douglas fir, tan oak, and redwood. This ride will take you past other traces of the once-busy logging industry. The Loma Prieta Mill site is now just a jumble of beams, which once were the foundation of a large redwood lumber mill. Two miles farther is the Top of the Incline, a structure built by the Molino Timber Company to haul split logs south to Aptos Creek using a steam donkey and narrow-gauge rail cars.

The Forest of Nisene Marks was the first property on the West Coast that the Nature Conservancy helped acquire for public use. In 1963, the Marks children, with assistance from the Nature Conservancy, donated the property to the state of California in memory of their mother, Nisene Marks.

This park also was the epicenter of the powerful October 17, 1989, earthquake that toppled the Nimitz Freeway in Oakland. The epicenter is located on the Aptos Creek Trail, which splits off of the Aptos Creek fire road. Bikes are not allowed on this trail, but hide yours in the bushes and hike the half mile to the sign locating the epicenter.

General location: About 4 miles south of Santa Cruz.
Elevation change: Aptos Creek Road leaves Soquel Drive at an elevation of about 200'. In 9 miles it climbs to 1,600' at Sand Point Overlook for a total elevation gain of approximately 1,400'.
Season: The road is open to riding year-round and is ideal from spring through late fall. Spring brings a multitude of wildflowers to the forest, including huckleberry, Western coltsfoot, fat Solomon's seal, gooseberry, thimbleberry, black-

RIDE 9 *APTOS CREEK FIRE ROAD / NISENE MARKS STATE PARK*

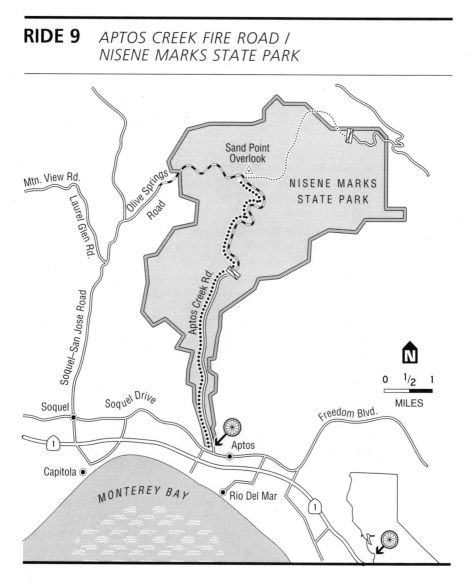

berry, and miner's lettuce. During the summer, this trail remains cool in the shade of overhanging trees. The weather often remains dry well into November, but winter rains can make this trail rather muddy. It's best to avoid wet winter rides because of trail erosion.

Services: No facilities are available at the park; all services are found in the town of Aptos or in Santa Cruz, 4 miles north of Aptos on CA 1. For camping, New Brighton State Beach is just one exit north on CA 1. There's also camping in the park at Westridge Trail Camp, but you must have advance reservations; call (408) 335-4598.

Hazards: Be sure to ride single file on the first section of this ride. The road is narrow and has two-way car traffic. Once on the trail, remember to watch for hikers and be sure they know you are behind them before passing. Also, watch for oncoming bike traffic.

Rescue index: Nisene Marks is well used by runners, walkers, and mountain bikers year-round. You'll often see at least 10 people on this ride, even in the middle of January, so make your way back towards the trailhead for assistance. The nearest phone is at the steel bridge over Aptos Creek.

Land status: California state park.

Maps: The park puts out a great map with lots of information for 50¢. The park rangers sell it but are not always around. The best way to get this map is to send 50¢ to park headquarters with your request; read just ahead for the address.

Finding the trail: Going south from Santa Cruz, take CA 1 to the Seacliff Beach/ Aptos exit. Turn left (east) and at the next intersection turn right onto Soquel Drive. You can start your ride here or continue driving a half mile to Aptos Creek Road. Turn left onto Aptos Creek Road and park in the turnout on the right, just past the railroad tracks.

Sources of additional information:

> The Forest of Nisene Marks State Park
> 101 North Big Trees Park Road
> Felton, CA 95018
> (408) 335-4598

Notes on the trail: The trail follows Aptos Creek Road, an old logging railroad grade that makes for easy, gentle riding. The roughest section is the first 2.2 miles, where you share the pothole-riddled gravel road with cars. At the gate, the rough gravel gives way to a smooth bed of redwood and pine needles all the way to Sand Point Overlook.

RIDE 10   *HENRY COWELL STATE PARK*

This seven-mile loop through the redwoods is an easy novice ride with some short, steep challenges. Trail conditions vary from pavement to sand, so expect to walk some brief stretches.

This park encompasses a variety of climate zones. Redwoods line the streams at the lower elevations, while the ridge tops rise to sun-loving chaparral. Between these zones is a mixed evergreen forest of live oak, madrone, Douglas fir, and

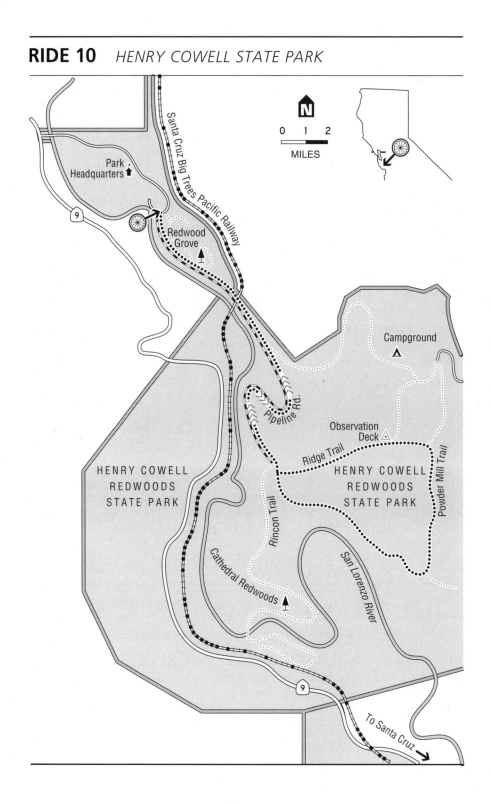

N

0   1   2
MILES

Santa Cruz Big Trees Pacific Railway

Park
Headquarters

9

Redwood
Grove

Campground

Pipeline Rd.

Observation
Deck

Ridge Trail

HENRY COWELL
REDWOODS
STATE PARK

HENRY COWELL
REDWOODS
STATE PARK

Powder Mill Trail

Rincon Trail

Cathedral Redwoods

San Lorenzo River

9

To Santa Cruz

Henry Cowell State Park is known for its magnificent redwoods.

ponderosa pine. Usually found above 3,000', the ponderosa pine is a rare species at this elevation, but you'll see an impressive stand around the observation deck.

The wildlife is as diverse as the plant life and you may see a squirrel, raccoon, Eastern fox, coyote, bobcat, or deer. Common birds here include Steller's jays, scrub jays, robins, juncos, chickadees, towhees, acorn woodpeckers, quail, and thrashers. Down near the streams, watch for mallards, blue herons, and kingfishers.

For thousands of years, redwoods dominated this area. The Ohlone Indians inhabited this environment until white settlers came west in droves seeking gold during the mid-1800s. Henry Cowell and his brother were among these "Forty-Niners," but instead of mining gold, they established a profitable drayage business. By the 1860s, Henry Cowell owned much of present-day Santa Cruz. In 1953, his last remaining heir deeded what is now Henry Cowell State Park to the state. To learn more about the Cowell family and the park, stop in at the nature center located at the trailhead. It has a good bookstore and is staffed by very helpful docents.

General location: On CA 9, 5 miles north of Santa Cruz.

Elevation change: The elevation of the parking area is close to 200'. The trail climbs to the observation deck at 800' for a total gain of 600'.

Season: Fall through late spring is the best time to ride here because the weather is cool and usually dry enough, and the park is much less crowded. The summer months bring many more visitors to the park and the trails can get very busy. If you plan to ride during the summer, avoid weekends and holidays, or get out on the trails early to avoid the crowds.

Services: The concession area at the trailhead sells food and also has water and rest rooms. Just north of the park, the little town of Felton has a grocery store and several restaurants. The coastal resort of Santa Cruz, just south on CA 9, offers numerous stores, restaurants, and hotels.

Hazards: On the far side of the observation deck, the whole trail consists of soft sand with a series of water bars to divert water off the trail. These water bars alternate with drop-offs that can make riding this section very tricky. Do not try to ride around them because you'll promote trail erosion and defeat the purpose of the water bars. You might prefer to walk your bike through this section, especially if you're new to mountain biking.

Rescue index: You are never farther than 3 miles from the trailhead and help is available at either the nature center or the concession area.

Land status: California state park.

Maps: A map is available for 50¢ at park headquarters.

Finding the trail: From CA 17 in Scotts Valley, take Mount Hermon Road 3 miles west to Graham Hill Road. Turn right and continue a half mile to CA 9 in the town of Felton. Turn left onto CA 9 and travel south 1 mile to the day-use entrance of Henry Cowell State Park.

From Santa Cruz, take CA 9 north for 5 miles and turn right into the park. Follow the main road to the concession area and parking lot. There's a $3 day-use fee per car.

Sources of additional information:

> Henry Cowell Redwoods State Park
> 101 North Big Trees Park Road
> Felton, CA 95018
> (408) 335-4598 (Office)
> (408) 438-2396 (Campground)
> (408) 335-9145 (District Headquarters)

Notes on the trail: After visiting the nature center, continue onto Pipeline Road for 2.2 miles to the Powder Mill Trail. Follow the Powder Mill Trail, staying left at all intersections, up to the Ridge Trail. Your ride crests at the observation deck on the summit. Continue down the other side of the hill, using caution through the sandy sections. Cross over Pipeline Road at the intersection and follow the Rincon Trail out to the Cathedral Redwoods Trail. Return to the parking area on Pipeline Road.

Monterey

RIDE 11 OLD COASTAL ROAD

This energetic 18.7-mile loop links the Old Coastal Road, a gravel highway, and the newer Pacific Coast Highway, CA 1. Starting on the old section of highway, you'll climb up and over three hills, one of them three miles long. The downhills are the trickiest where runoff has created ruts in the road.

You'll ride through several distinct changes of scenery. The first mile passes through dry hillsides of brush. At the bottom of the canyon, the road follows a stream and surrounds you with lush ferns and redwoods. If you're riding on a hot day, you'll appreciate being shaded on the uphill. The top of the road breaks out of the trees into open grassland with a few scattered oaks and a spectacular view of both the blue Pacific and the coastal headlands.

General location: Fourteen miles south of Monterey.

Elevation change: The ride starts at 276', then climbs to 400' at the top of the first hill. The elevation drops down to 200' at Sierra Creek before reaching 1,000' on the second hill summit. Another great downhill whisks you to the Little Sur River at 120', and back up you go to the third and final summit at 942'. The last descent brings you back to CA 1, about 8 miles south of where you parked.

Season: Riding in this area is possible throughout the year due to the temperate Mediterranean coastal climate. Spring wildflowers are beautiful in the meadows along this road; California golden poppy and iris sometimes reveal themselves as early as January. The summer months pack CA 1 with tourists, so traffic on this section is often heavy. Fall usually remains sunny along the central coast, while much of the north coast may be under storm clouds.

Services: There are no facilities available on this ride. However, at the end of the Old Coastal Road, you can turn south on CA 1 and in 3 miles reach a small convenience store and restaurant. This detour adds 6 miles to the loop, but after a hard ride, a cold drink in 3 miles might sound better than a hot car in 8. For a large selection of hotels, restaurants, and grocery stores, go north to Monterey. For camping, travel south to Pfeiffer Big Sur State Park, (408) 667-2315.

Hazards: Keep your speed in control on the downhills, for some sections are rocky and rutted from runoff.

Rescue index: There are houses on this road but no promises that anyone will

The Old Coastal Road drops into wooded areas then climbs up into open grassland.

be home. The nearest help would be on CA 1, where you might be able to flag down a motorist. The nearest public phone is at the convenience store 3 miles south of the southern end of this ride.

Land status: State highway and access road.

Maps: Any reasonably detailed highway map of the Big Sur/Monterey area will show the Old Coastal Road.

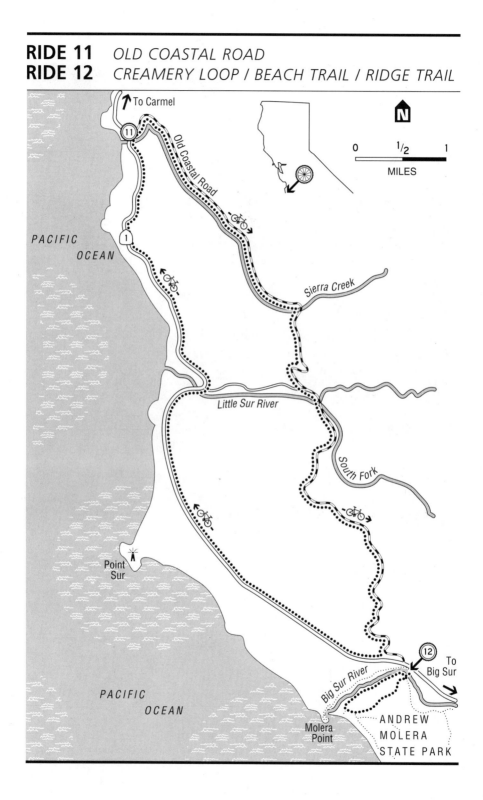

Finding the trail: From the Carmel River Bridge on CA 1, it's 12.5 miles to an unnamed bridge, followed by another bridge in a half mile. Just before the second bridge, the Old Coastal Road leaves the highway on your left. Park your car on the west side of CA 1 or at the beginning of the Old Coastal Road.

Sources of additional information:

Aquarian Bicycles
486 Washington
Monterey, CA 93940
(408) 375-2144

RIDE 12 *CREAMERY TRAIL, BEACH TRAIL, AND RIDGE TRAIL*

Andrew Molera State Park, a small beachfront reserve, has several short trails to explore via mountain bike. The rides vary in length from two to six miles and can be done in any combination, as well as in conjunction with the Old Coastal Road, which ends across the highway (CA 1) from Andrew Molera State Park.

There are two level loops around the Creamery and Beach Trails, each two miles long, and a six-mile loop around the Ridge Trail that has a two-mile climb. The tough climb is moderated by the beautiful views of the ocean, which provide a good excuse to stop and look around. All the trails are hard-packed dirt, except at the beach where they turn to sand. Riding in this area is therefore easy, because little technical skill is needed on these smooth trails.

Along the Beach Trail and the Creamery Trail, you'll encounter a stream-bank environment, with trees such as willow, red alder, sycamore, and cottonwood. The birds you may see include the blue heron, water ouzel, and kingfisher. The meadow in the middle of the Creamery Trail grows thick with wild grasses, vetch, oats, foxtail, mustard, and poppies. As you climb the Ridge Trail through the meadows and into the mixed forest of redwood, canyon oak, coast live oak, and madrone, watch for birds of prey. The red-tailed hawk is the most common, but the Cooper's hawk, black-shouldered hawk, barn owl, and great horned owl also are seen here.

The ride up the Ridge Trail is magnificent. Even if you don't complete the entire loop, the views are worth the effort. Another highlight is the Headlands Trail. Lock up your bike and walk up to Molera Point; from here, you sometimes can see otters, seals, sea lions, whales, and a variety of ocean birds.

General location: Twenty miles south of Monterey on CA 1.
Elevation change: The parking lot is just above sea level. The Beach Trail and the Creamery Trail are level, while the Ridge Trail gains a total of 1,000' in 2 miles.
Season: Temperatures along the coast are mild year-round. Usually the ocean

Just one of the many breathtaking views of the coast from Andrew Molera State Park.

breeze keeps the air comfortable even on the hottest of days. Spring can bring rain but also a beautiful array of wildflowers. The summer months bring heavier use to the park as the weather becomes consistently warmer. January is the height of the gray whale migration; a great spot to watch for spouts is at the end of the Headlands Trail on Molera Point.

Services: Three miles south on CA 1 are several small hotels, a restaurant, and a convenience store. Here also is the nearest public phone. For a wide selection of facilities, go north to Monterey. There's a walk-in campground here at Andrew Molera; additional camping is available south of here at Pfeiffer Big Sur State Park, (408) 667-2315.

Hazards: If you plan to play on the beach, be extremely watchful for large sleeper waves, which can sweep you into the ocean.

Rescue index: You are never more than 3 miles from CA 1, where there's steady traffic to flag down if emergency assistance is needed.

Land status: Andrew Molera State Park.

Maps: A pamphlet containing the history and a map of the park is available from any ranger or at Pfeiffer Big Sur State Park nearby.

Finding the trail: Andrew Molera State Park is located 22 miles south of Carmel on CA 1. Follow signs for Andrew Molera and turn right into the gravel parking area, where all the loop trails begin. There's a $3 day-use fee.

Sources of additional information:

Aquarian Bicycles
486 Washington
Monterey, CA 93940
(408) 375-2144

Andrew Molera State Park
c/o Pfeiffer Big Sur State Park
Big Sur, CA 93920
(408) 667-2315

Santa Rosa

RIDE 13 BEAR VALLEY TRAIL / POINT REYES

This eight-mile loop is a very easy ride, suitable for all abilities. It starts at the Bear Valley Visitor Center, which is an excellent resource for information on the surrounding area. The Bear Valley Trail is a wide gravel path that has very little elevation change. As a bonus, park and lock your bike to the rack at the end of the bike trail and hike the last half mile out to the coast, where there are both cliffs and beaches to explore. It's a great place to bring a picnic lunch.

General location: At the Point Reyes National Seashore headquarters near the town of Olema, one hour north of San Francisco.

Elevation change: There's a total 100′ elevation gain, which you climb in the first 4 miles.

Season: This region has a Mediterranean climate, characterized by a wet season (October–March) and a dry season (April–September). There's a good chance that the weather will be foggy and windy out on the peninsula near the ocean, so be prepared for sun and fog both.

Services: There are rest rooms, pay phones, and water at the Visitor Center. All services are available in Point Reyes Station. Camping is available on Point Reyes; check at the Bear Valley Visitor Center. Olema Ranch Campground is a nearby private campground with showers.

Hazards: Please remember to slow down and alert hikers when passing them on this multi-use trail. If you expect to be away from your bike at any time, carry a lock and secure your bike to the rack at the end of the trail.

Rescue index: Help is available at the Visitor Center at the beginning of the Bear Valley Trail.

Land status: Point Reyes National Seashore.

Maps: Available at the Visitor Center.

Finding the trail: The Bear Valley Visitor Center is located .6 miles west of CA 1, the Shoreline Highway, on Bear Valley Road. Follow signs from CA 1 to the Visitor Center. Coming from the south, the turn is just past the town of Olema. Turn again at the red barn towards the Visitor Center and park in the large parking area. The trail starts at the far end of the parking area.

Sources of additional information: Point Reyes National Seashore headquarters, (415) 663-1092.

RIDE 13 *BEAR VALLEY TRAIL / POINT REYES*

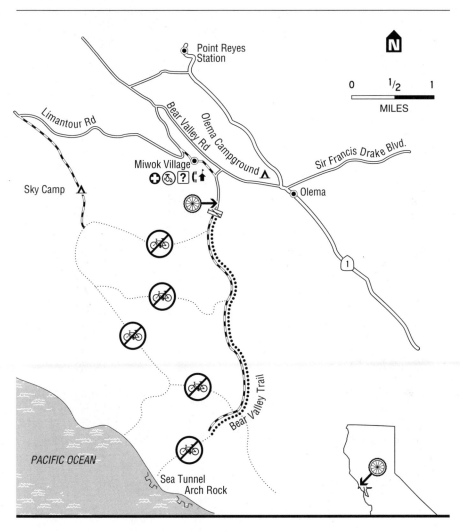

The terrain on Bear Valley Trail is easily navigated.

RIDE 14   *ANNADEL STATE PARK*

This incredible park just outside of Santa Rosa has 35 miles of great mountain bike trails and 5,000 acres of rolling hills. You can create many combinations of rides from 3 to 20 miles long. All the trails are wide dirt or gravel roads; some (like the Rough Go Trail and Two Quarry Trail) are rougher than others. A good first ride takes you on a loop up around Lake Ilsanjo and Ledson Marsh. The climbing is gradual and the trails are smooth.

The tremendous ecological diversity of this park—with meadows, Douglas fir forests, and chaparral areas—makes it a wonderful place to explore if you enjoy wild plants and animals.

General location: Approximately 9 miles east of Santa Rosa on CA 12.
Elevation change: Your trailhead begins in the parking lot at 400', climbing to 800' at Lake Ilsanjo and a high of 1,400' at Buick Meadows. You drop down into Ledson Marsh at 1,200' and then climb back up to Buick Meadows before the long descent back to the parking lot. Total elevation gain is 1,200'.
Season: You'll want to dress in layers, as summer temperatures range anywhere from 50 to 90 degrees while winter temperatures range from 40 to 70 degrees. Rainfall averages 30 inches per year, most of it during the winter and into the spring months of April and May. If it has recently rained, take a break from mountain biking and give the trails a chance to dry out.
Services: You'll find water and rest rooms at the parking area at the end of Channel Drive. All services are available in Santa Rosa. You can camp at Spring Lake County Park, on the northeast side of Annadel Park.
Hazards: Watch for rocks and gullies in the trail from the spring runoff. Also, this is a multi-use park so please use extreme caution when passing horses and hikers. On August 20, 1989, a horse had to be destroyed due to injury received after being spooked by three mountain bikers. The cyclists scared the horse when they sped by shouting, "We're coming through!" The horse threw the rider, the saddle slid to the side, and the animal's right hoof got caught in the stirrup, causing it to fall and break its leg. With the increase in cyclists using the park, the following guidelines have been established to help prevent accidents from occuring:

- Yield to horses and hikers.
- Announce yourself and ask permission before passing.
- Slow down on blind corners.
- Keep speed to 15 mph or less.
- Stay on marked trails.

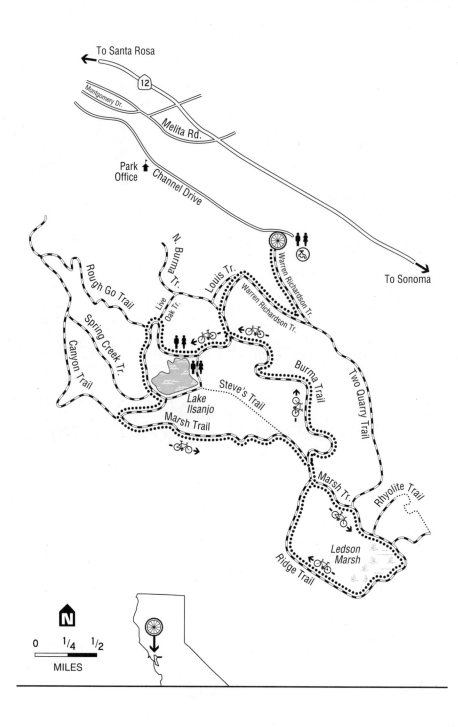

Annadel State Park has many wide trails that hikers, horses, and cyclists can share.

Rescue index: Help is available at the park office on Channel Drive or at Warrack Hospital on Hoen Avenue. Both of these are on the Annadel State Park map.
Land status: California state park.
Maps: Annadel State Park maps are available for 75¢ each from a vending machine in front of the park office on Channel Drive.
Finding the trail: Coming east from Santa Rosa, take CA 12 for about 9 miles. Take a right onto Los Alamos Road, then turn right again on Melita Road and immediately left on Montgomery Drive. Watch for Channel Drive on your left; follow it to the park office where you can purchase your map and pay the day-use fee. Continue on Channel Drive until it ends in a parking lot, where the Warren Richardson Trail begins.

Sources of additional information:

> Annadel State Park
> 6201 Channel Drive
> Santa Rosa, CA 95409
> (707) 539-3911

Notes on the trail: Starting from the parking area at the end of Channel Drive, take the Warren Richardson Trail up to Lake Ilsanjo. Go to your right around the lake, turning left onto the Rough Go Trail. After crossing the dam, go right at the next intersection onto the Canyon Trail. Then turn left at the Marsh Trail for another climb up to Buick Meadows. Stay on the Marsh Trail, which takes you down to Ledson Marsh. Follow this trail as it loops around the marsh and climb up the Ridge Trail, which loops back to the Marsh Trail. Turn right onto the Burma Trail to head back to Lake Ilsanjo and the Warren Richardson Trail, which returns to the parking lot.

All intersections are signed, so take along your map and you shouldn't have any problems.

RIDE 15 *SUGARLOAF RIDGE STATE PARK*

This is a short, tough ride with plenty of elevation gain. The uphill part of this six-mile loop is on pavement; you come back down on gravel roads. Most riders find that they have to take breaks on the uphill or even walk some sections if their gearing isn't low enough. Once at the top, however, the views of San Francisco and the Sierra Nevada Range on a clear day are well worth the grind.

General location: Approximately 15 miles east of Santa Rosa on CA 12.
Elevation change: The Visitor Center is located at 1,200'. Your trail crests at 2,729' on the summit of Bald Mountain, for a total elevation gain of 1,529'.
Season: Temperatures fluctuate widely here, from 50 to 90 degrees in summer and from 40 to 70 degrees in winter. Rains can be heavy during the winter and spring, even as late as May. Dressing in layers is your best bet for staying comfortable.
Services: All services are available in Santa Rosa or Kenwood. Camping is available within the park.
Hazards: Other than the usual mountain biking challenges, watch out for poison oak. You can recognize it by its leaves, which grow in clusters of three that are glossy green in spring and brilliant red in late summer and fall. People have various reactions to skin contact with this plant, ranging from mild, localized itching at the contact site to severe swelling, itching, and blistering all over the

RIDE 15 *SUGARLOAF RIDGE STATE PARK*

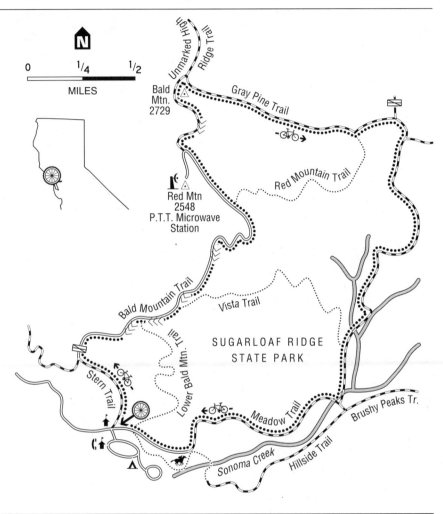

body. Even if you don't usually notice plants, this is one you should be able to recognize for your own safety.

Rescue index: Return to the Visitor Center for assistance.

Land status: California state park.

Maps: Sugarloaf Ridge State Park maps are available at the Visitor Center for 75¢ each.

Finding the trail: The park is located 3.5 miles east of CA 12 in Kenwood on

Don't forget to pick up your feet when you cross Sonoma Creek in Sugarloaf Ridge State Park!

Adobe Canyon Road. The Visitor Center will be on your left. Buy your map here and continue for another quarter of a mile to the trailhead and parking area on the left-hand side of the road.

Sources of additional information:

Sugarloaf Ridge State Park
2605 Adobe Canyon Road
Kenwood, CA 95452
(707) 833-5712

Notes on the trail: This ride is interesting because of its challenging climbs, sparsely used trails, and spectacular views. You'll climb Bald Mountain on a paved service road that is steep enough to make the average rider walk most of the way. Once at the top of Bald Mountain, named for its smooth, rounded, rocky cap, you can see San Francisco's skyline to the south and the Sierra Nevada Mountains to the east. Even when the sky isn't clear enough to view these distant features, the beautiful geometric patterns of the nearby Napa Valley vineyards are usually visible just to the east.

Closely read the map and signposts at the summit, where there's a junction that can be confusing. Just before you reach the top of Bald Mountain, there is an unmarked trail off to your left; do not take that turn. Instead, continue another 50 feet to an intersection where a right-hand trail will take you to the top of the peaks and a left-hand trail will be your route down the mountain. The trip down takes about 45 minutes. For approximately a mile, you'll be riding on the ridge, which is recognizable by its undulating, rolling terrain. The trail then follows Sonoma Creek and crosses it just before opening up into a meadow. The trail quickly changes to a gravel road that takes you back over the creek and down into the service area of the park, where the rangers live. From here, follow the gravel road back to your car at the trailhead.

Mount Saint Helena

RIDE 16 NORTH AND SOUTH PEAKS

This short but steady grind has some very steep but rewarding sections, especially the final climb to the North Peak. It's an out-and-back ride of 5.4 miles to
the South Peak and 6.7 miles to the North Peak, for an 11- to 14-mile round-trip.
The trail is a fire road consisting of loose dirt and gravel, occasionally with large
rocks and deep grooves that are best avoided.

Starting in an evergreen forest, you climb up to drier hillsides of madrone
and chaparral; watch for interesting volcanic rock formations here. Reaching an
obvious summit, look for a small wooden marker on the left that shows the way
to either peak. You can continue straight toward the North Peak, where there's
an abandoned fire lookout, or you can take a sharp left turn up to the South
Peak, where there's a gazebo and a radio tower.

Views from either summit are spectacular. On a clear day, you can see the
Palisades, all of Napa and Pope Valleys, parts of Alexander Valley, numerous
lakes, the Bay area, the ocean, and even Mount Shasta and Mount Lassen to the
northeast—some 190 miles away. Literary buffs will enjoy the one-mile walk up
the hiking trail from the parking area to view where Robert Louis Stevenson's
cabin once stood. In 1880, he spent his honeymoon here. The hiking trail continues on up the mountain for another half mile, then connects with the fire road
to the top.

General location: About 8 miles north of Calistoga on CA 29 in Robert Louis
Stevenson State Park.
Elevation change: The parking area is at 2,300', the North Peak is at 4,343',
and the South Peak is at 4,000'. Total elevation gain ranges from 1,700' to a
little over 2,000', depending on your route.
Season: Mount Saint Helena offers all-season riding, with more climatic variety
than you'll find at lower elevations. In summer, it's blazing hot since the road
is dusty and exposed to the sun. Temperatures can reach over 100 degrees, so
carry extra water. In winter, there are many clear days but they get cold. The
road usually has wet spots and sometimes patches of ice and snow. Dress warmly
because the wind at the top really has a bite.
Services: Calistoga is the closest town south of this ride. Located at the north
end of the Napa Valley, it has all the services you'll need. Favorite restaurants

RIDE 16 *NORTH AND SOUTH PEAKS*

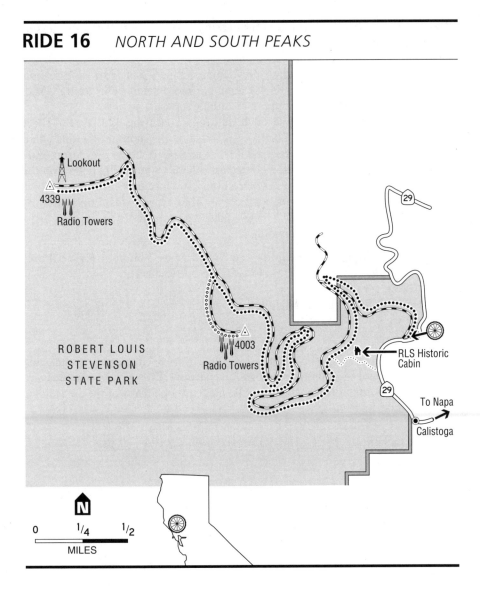

include the Calistoga Drive-In, which has great Mexican food, and the English Pub, serving Red Tail Ale.

Hazards: The fire road has many switchbacks that create blind turns, so be alert. On weekdays this area usually is deserted except for an occasional utility truck that uses the fire road. Watch for trucks on the descent, as well as for hikers and other cyclists, especially on weekends in the summer.

If you wander off the trail, keep an eye out for poison oak.

Rescue index: There's no phone at the parking area, so you're basically on your own unless you can flag down somebody for assistance.

Land status: Robert Louis Stevenson State Park.

Maps: A good map of this whole area, *Wine Country and North Bay Counties,* is available in most stores in this area. For more detail, refer to the USGS topographic map for Calistoga in the 15-minute series.

Finding the trail: Take CA 29 through Calistoga, following signs for Lakeport and Middletown. Seven miles north of Calistoga, at the summit of a long climb up the side of Mount Saint Helena, turn off at Robert Louis Stevenson State Park. Park your car on either side of the road; there's a large dirt pulloff on the right side of the road and a smaller one on the left. Once on your bike, continue down CA 29 (towards Lakeport) for a couple of hundred yards. Look carefully on the left side of the road for a metal, single-bar gate and a fire road. This is your road to the top of the mountain.

Sources of additional information: There's no ranger station at Robert Louis Stevenson Park. For more information, contact the rangers at:

Bothe-Napa Valley State Park
3801 North Saint Helena Highway
Calistoga, CA 94515
(707) 942-4575

Brian Ivanoff researched this ride for this publication. Brian grew up in the Napa Valley and recently graduated from the University of California at Santa Barbara. An avid mountain biker and rock climber, he's explored many of the areas in the wine country.

Van Damme State Park

RIDE 17 *PYGMY FOREST*

You can start this ride in Mendocino for a 13.3-mile loop or at Van Damme Beach for a shorter ride of 7.5 miles. Beginners will enjoy riding over paved trails with very little elevation gain, except for a short, steep climb up to the Pygmy Forest. From Mendocino, CA 1 follows gently rolling terrain along the Pacific coastline, revealing superb ocean views that are capped off with a breezy downhill to the park entrance. At Van Damme State Park, the trail follows the Little River through Fern Canyon. The canyon is appropriately named for its lush growth of ferns, including the five-fingered, bird's foot, lady, licorice, sword, and deer species. Fern Canyon also is home to redwoods, red alders, bigleaf maples, Douglas firs, and an understory of Oregon grape and berry bushes.

At the top of the loop is a short walk through the Pygmy Forest, a miniature forest of coastal cypress resulting from a unique combination of geology, soils, and climate. A nutrient-poor, highly acidic topsoil, above a layer of dense red hardpan that resists root penetration, severely restricts the growth of the trees located here. These soil conditions occur in patches so that the pygmy trees, some as old as sixty years, grow just a few feet tall and less than an inch in diameter alongside the normal coastal cypress.

The Fern Canyon Trail was once an old skid road used by ox teams to haul logs down to the mouth of the river, where a lumber mill once stood. Charles Van Damme, who gave the park its name, was born in Little River and grew up to be a San Francisco ferry-boat tycoon. He purchased 40 acres of river frontage, which was given to the state after his death. Van Damme State Park now totals 1,831 acres and runs five miles back into Mendocino headlands.

General location: Three miles south of Mendocino on CA 1.
Elevation change: The park entrance is at 50'; the top of the loop is 560' at the Pygmy Forest. Your total elevation gain is 510' for the loop within the park.
Season: A ride for all seasons. The whole path is paved so there's no problem with muddy trails. Winter is cold and wet, and spring is generally misty, though March is the best time for whale-watching. Summer is ideal because temperatures near the coast remain comfortable for riding in spite of blazing heat inland.

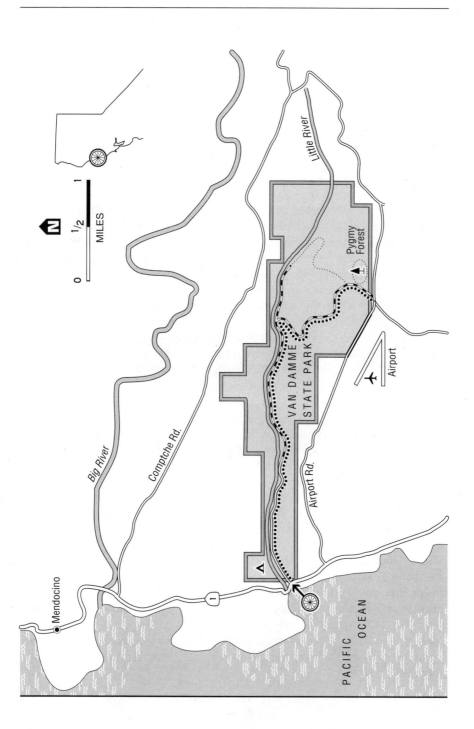

Pack a towel so you can take a dip at Van Damme Beach after riding the loop through the park, and before your 3-mile ride back to Mendocino.

Services: You'll find water, rest rooms, and a phone at the park entrance. All services are located in Mendocino, a beautiful little town full of historic sites, bed-and-breakfasts, and delicious restaurants. Camping is available in Van Damme State Park.

Hazards: Always use caution when riding where there's car traffic. CA 1, the Pacific Coast Highway, is busy (especially in summer) but has an adequate shoulder to ride on. If you stop to explore Van Damme Beach, respect the rough surf and large waves.

Rescue index: You're never far from help on this ride. Return to the park entrance for assistance.

Land status: California state park.

Maps: Any good road map that includes Mendocino County will show all roads on this ride except the 1.2-mile section between Fern Canyon and the Pygmy Forest.

Finding the trail: Park your car along CA 1 in the town Mendocino for the longer loop. For the shorter ride, drive south on CA 1 for 2.9 miles and park on the right in the Van Damme Beach parking lot.

Sources of additional information:

Van Damme State Park
P.O. Box 440
Mendocino, CA 95437
(707) 937-5804

Notes on the trail: From Mendocino, turn south onto CA 1. Watch for a left turn after a nice downhill into Van Damme State Park. Continue straight back into the park and follow signs up to the Pygmy Forest. The steepest section is the Logging Road Trail, running from the Fern Canyon Trail to the Pygmy Forest. At the entrance to the Pygmy Forest, lock your bike and walk the short nature loop. From here, you'll ride mostly downhill on the Little River-Airport Road back to CA 1. Turn right onto CA 1 back to Mendocino.

Lakeport

RIDE 18 *BOGGS MOUNTAIN STATE FOREST*

Numerous trail combinations, ranging from three to twelve miles long, are possible in this little paradise. I have no specific recommendations, but starting at the fire station gives you a choice of paved roads, gravel roads, or single-track trails.

The new single-tracks that weave through the woods were cut recently by Bob McDonell, a fire fighter, for mountain bikes. His crew uses these trails for running and mountain biking in the summer to stay in shape for fighting fires. The single-tracks are unsigned and may be hard to follow, but the forest is criss-crossed with gravel roads that are numbered at intersections. If you carry your map, you won't get lost. Although most of the roads through the forest are gravel, there are paved roads on the southwest and northeast sides. If you tire of gravel and dirt, you can ride one of these paved roads back to the park entrance.

The Boggs Mountain State Forest is named after a Lake County pioneer, Henry C. Boggs. He owned much of this area between 1878 and 1884, using it for logging and for grazing cattle. In 1949, the state bought this tract in order to experiment with and demonstrate various forestry practices. As you ride through the forest, you'll notice that some areas have been thinned, cut, or burned in efforts to promote continual growth. Trees here consist mostly of Douglas fir, ponderosa pine, and other mixed conifers. Views of the surrounding hills are beautiful from some of the higher points in the forest.

General location: Approximately 22 miles south of Lakeport on CA 175, or 26 miles north of Calistoga.
Elevation change: The forest entrance is at 3,000′ and the highest point in the park rises to just over 3,600′ at the south end. Total elevation gain (out-and-back) is usually 1,000′, but will vary depending on the length of your ride.
Season: The best time for riding is April through mid-December. The spring months are the prettiest, with many wildflowers and dogwood trees in bloom. At 3,000′, this area stays cooler than the surrounding valleys, but morning rides are best to avoid the summer heat. Late fall and winter bring cool, clear days and fun riding when snow and mud are not present.
Services: Water is available from a hose next to the forestry buildings, near the parking areas. There are no other facilities available at Boggs Mountain State

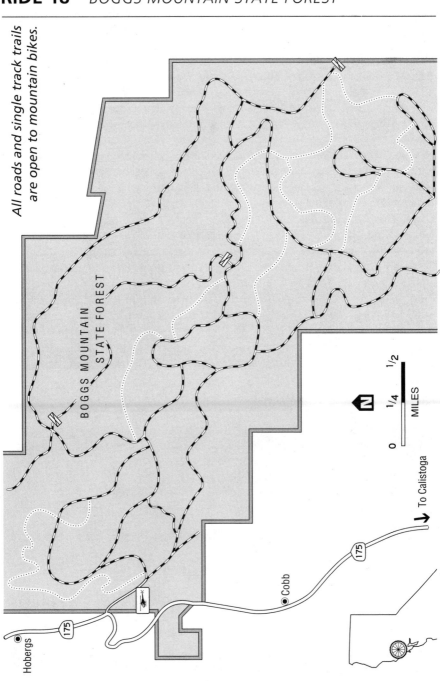

All roads and single track trails are open to mountain bikes.

BOGGS MOUNTAIN STATE FOREST

N

0   1/4   1/2
MILES

To Calistoga

175

Cobb

175

Hobergs

Forest. The small town of Cobb is located just south of the entrance and has a grocery store, a post office, and a restaurant. For more options, go south to Middletown or north to Lakeport.

Hazards: Boggs Mountain State Forest is open for deer hunting from mid-August through September, and though the woods are lovely this time of year, it's probably safest to avoid them. If you feel that you absolutely must ride during deer season, wear plenty of safety orange. There's also a squirrel season through most of the summer but it has not been a problem so far for other people using the forest.

Rescue index: The nearest help is located at the heliport located just inside the entrance to the forest. In the summer, the helicopter crew is on call for other emergencies so they are not always available. Continue to the town of Cobb if there's no one at the heliport.

Land status: California state forest.

Maps: Boggs Mountain State Forest has a free map of the park that can be obtained upon request from the California Department of Forestry. It does not, however, show the recent mountain bike trail additions. For topography, see the USGS 7.5-minute quad for Whispering Pines.

Finding the trail: From Lakeport, take CA 29 south a little over ten and a half miles to CA 175. Continue south on CA 175 for another 14.2 miles. Just past the town of Hoberg, turn left into the state forest. (If you reach the town of Cobb, you've gone too far.) Follow the sign for the State Fire Station; you'll see no sign for Boggs Mountain until after you turn off CA 175. Park your car across the road from the heliport.

Sources of additional information:

Steve Sayers or Bob McDonell
California Department of Forestry
P.O. Box 839
Cobb, CA 95426
(707) 928-4378

Brian and Norma Aldeghi
Bicycle Rack
350 North Main Street
Lakeport, CA 95453
(707) 263-1200

Many thanks to Steve Sayers and Bob McDonell for creating more areas for mountain bikes.

RIDE 19 *LAKEPORT TOLL ROAD*

This is a 17.3- or 23.5-mile ride over paved and gravel roads. The longer mileage is if you ride from Lakeport rather than Highland Springs, but both mileages assume that someone is picking you up in Hopland. (True to its name, there's beer worth sampling in town.)

From Lakeport, you'll ride on paved roads through walnut orchards and grape vineyards. At Highland Springs Reservoir, stop to rest on the grassy meadow that surrounds the reservoir before the gravel begins. From here, it's a little less than seven miles to the high point of this ride. The slopes dry out as you rise; oaks and open grassland dominate the hillsides. The road follows Highland Springs Creek for approximately three miles beyond the reservoir. Then it leaves the drainage to climb up and over the summit. A quick descent brings you back down to vineyards and farmland. Turn left onto CA 175 to Hopland.

If you enjoy wines, a couple of side trips will take you to well-known wineries. To see the Kendall-Jackson Winery, take a right onto Mathews Road from Highland Springs Road; return to Highland Springs to continue your ride. Near Hopland, watch for the Fetzer Winery on the left.

If wine doesn't interest you, perhaps a cold beer at the end of the ride will. The Hopland Brewery, famous for its Red Tail Ale, is on your right as you ride through town. This is a great place to meet your shuttle back to Lakeport.

General location: Southwest of Lakeport.
Elevation change: Highland Springs is at 1,460', the summit is at 2,400', and Hopland is at 600'. Your total elevation gain is 940' and you'll go down a total of 1,800'.
Season: The best seasons for riding are spring through late fall, although the roads always are busiest during the summer.
Services: Water and rest rooms are available on the east side of the Highland Springs Reservoir. All services are available in the town of Lakeport. For bicycle needs, see Brian and Norma Aldeghi at the Bicycle Rack on Main Street.
Hazards: Use caution on the descent via the Old Toll Road—it's narrow and carries local traffic, so keep to the right and don't cut corners. The roads are busy on the way out of Lakeport and into Hopland, so stay as far to the right as you can.
Rescue index: The gravel section of this ride is used year-round by locals. In the summer, it's busier with campers accessing the popular Sheldon Creek Campground in the Cow Mountain Recreation Area. The chances of someone passing you on the road usually are good.
Land status: State and local public roads; Cow Mountain Recreation Area.
Maps: Any regional map of Lake and Mendocino Counties should show the

RIDE 19 *LAKEPORT TOLL ROAD*

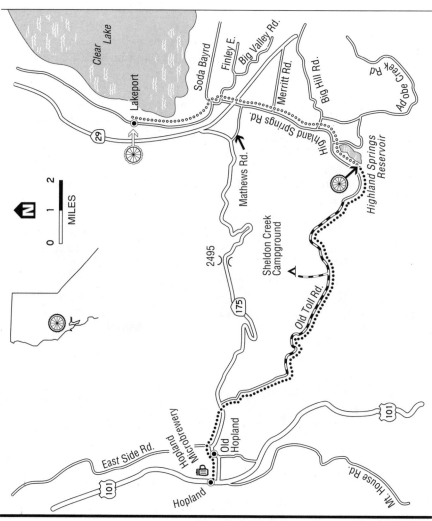

Old Toll Road. See also the USGS 7.5-minute quads for both Highland Springs and Hopland.

Finding the trail: For the 23.5-mile ride, start in downtown Lakeport. Ideally, a driver who'll pick you up in Hopland can drop you off in Lakeport. For the shorter ride, start at Highland Springs Reservoir. To get there, take North Main Street south out of Lakeport for 3.2 miles. Turn right onto Big Valley Road, and in .3 miles, veer right again onto Highland Springs Road. At this point look for a sign on the right that says "Sheldon Creek Campground: 10 miles" and "Hopland-Lakeport Highway: 20 miles." Stay right and follow the road as it loops around the reservoir. Park your car on the west side of the reservoir.

Sources of additional information:

Brian and Norma Aldeghi
Bicycle Rack
350 North Main Street
Lakeport, CA 95453
(707) 263-1200

Redwoods

RIDE 20 *PRAIRIE CREEK REDWOODS STATE PARK*

This generally easy 13.3-mile loop starts at the Prairie Creek Visitor Center. The route to Fern Canyon has wide, gentle grades over smooth dirt roads. At Fern Canyon, the road turns to single-track with a few obstacles. The toughest section is the half-mile climb up the Ossagon Trail, where most riders will need to get off and push their bikes.

The ride starts on a jogging path that is partly a gravel road and partly a wide path with a soft cushion of fallen needles. The path takes you to Davison Road, a smooth gravel road all the way to Fern Canyon, where the road becomes a single-track trail. This trail has logs and other small obstacles, and some short sandy sections. The trail splits into two paths, one through open grasslands and the other along the base of steep Gold Bluffs. Many elk live along the base of the bluffs, so you may have to change trails to avoid them. The Ossagon Trail follows an old roadbed that was closed by the park because it was used by poachers. The poachers would hunt the elk in this area and sneak down the Ossagon Trail when the rangers would come down Davison Road to catch them.

Once on the Ossagon Trail, the path widens again and becomes smooth but steep. As you push your bike up the hill, you may wonder why I didn't have you do the loop in reverse. Coming down this hill is pretty scary and people often end up walking down. By riding the loop as described, you can walk up this steep section and enjoy the smooth downhill on the jogging path and Davison Road at the beginning of the loop. After the intersection with US 101, it's 5.7 paved miles back to Prairie Creek Visitor Center.

Redwoods surround you as you start your ride at Prairie Creek. The jogging path and Davison Road drop down through cool, shaded hillsides of second-growth forest. The road runs along the bottom of the Gold Bluffs and virtually puts you on the beach, with the wild surf crashing on the sand. The Ossagon Trail enters alder forests as you climb away from the beach; near the top, you pedal past the ancient redwoods that line the road back to Prairie Creek.

This loop is not only exceedingly scenic, but rich in historical lore as well. The area around Fern Canyon was the focus of intensive gold mining from 1850 to 1920. The gold had been deposited by the Klamath River, which once entered the sea here. Many fortune-seekers were discouraged by the difficulty of separating the gold from the sand and gravel mixed in with it, but a few hardy souls stuck around. These miners lived just north of Fern Canyon in Lincoln Prairie. All signs of their industry have since disappeared. Before the miners, the Yurok Indians lived under these cliffs; one of their villages was located on Ossagon Prairie. Now the only year-round occupants are the Roosevelt elk, which may appear to be quite tame, but please give them plenty of space.

General location: About 30 miles south of Crescent City.

Elevation change: The ride begins at 120' and is mostly level to Davison Road, where it climbs to 200' before dropping down to 80' along the base of Gold Bluffs. The Ossagon Trail climbs up to 920' at its intersection with US 101 and gradually returns to 120' at Prairie Creek Visitor Center. Total elevation gain is 920'.

Season: The coastal redwood climate is mild, so riding is possible throughout the year. The best months are September and October, when the weather is usually dry and warm, although occasional rainstorms may blow in. November through March are the rainiest months but still have sunny days; if there hasn't been much rain recently, the trails might be dry enough to ride. April and May are the greenest months, showcasing wildflowers from the winter's rain. Strong winds often occur, but fog is less common than in June, July, and August. During these three months, the weather might be sunny and hot inland while the coast is smothered by thick, damp fog. (That's what makes the climate ideal for the redwoods). These also are the most crowded months for tourism.

Services: Rest rooms, water, and a phone are available at the Visitor Center. The nearest town is Orick, just 7 miles south of the Prairie Creek Visitor Center. It has a small grocery, a few restaurants, and a post office. For more variety, go north to Crescent City or south to Eureka.

Hazards: The two greatest hazards on this ride are the elk and the traffic on US 101. The elk aren't shy of humans but this doesn't mean that they're tame. They will chase you if you get too close! Give them a wide berth if you encounter them on your bike, which may happen down in the Gold Bluffs Beach area. If elk are in your path you may have to walk your bike off the trail to avoid getting too close.

Stay to the right on US 101; traffic moves very fast and visibility is limited. The highway has a two-foot-wide shoulder that feels much narrower when a logging truck zooms by. If traffic is backing up behind you, please stop your bike on the shoulder and allow others to pass.

Rescue index: Rangers patrol these areas during the summer, but during the rest of the year, your nearest source of assistance would be the motorists on US 101.

Land status: California state park.

Maps: *Trails: Redwood National Park, California State Parks,* a small map of hiking trails, is available at visitor centers throughout the northern coastal redwoods region for one dollar.

Finding the trail: Prairie Creek Visitor Center is just 9 miles north of Orick and approximately 30 miles south of Crescent City on US 101. There's a $3 day-use

Watch for elk in Prairie Creek Redwoods.

parking fee per car. As you enter the park, the Visitor Center is on your right. To get the most out of your ride, be sure to explore the exhibits there. If the parking lot is full, continue straight toward the campground, where there's additional parking on the right-hand side of the road.

Sources of additional information:

Prairie Creek Redwoods State Park
(707) 488-2171

Redwood National Park
1111 Second Street
Crescent City, CA 95531
(707) 464-6101 (24-hour information line)

Notes on the trail: From the Prairie Creek Visitor Center, ride toward the campground. Continue straight past roads leaving to the right and left. When the road dead-ends there's a gate; go around it and continue on the trail. Go straight where Elk Prairie Trail goes left and start watching for little yellow signs with a jogger symbol. You'll come to another gate; go around it and turn right onto a gravel road. There'll be another gate to skirt around and soon you'll turn left off of the road and back onto the jogging path. From this point, it's about 2 miles to Davison Road.

At the 2-mile mark, a sign tells joggers to turn around but your trail continues onto Davison Road. Turn right and continue straight at the fee station. It's about 4 miles from here to Fern Canyon, and there are three stream crossings. The third crossing is Home Creek, which flows out of Fern Canyon. After you cross the creek, the road turns to single-track. In less than a mile from Fern Canyon, the Boat Creek Trail goes right but you stay left. Your trail soon splits: one fork goes through the prairie and the other hugs the base of the bluffs. Ahead, these paths will converge briefly before splitting again. Stay to the left after the paths split. Watch out for elk in the spruce grove on the right.

If you want, you can take the short side trail on the right that leads to Gold Dust Falls, a small stream that drops about 100' to disappear into the sand. A second waterfall lies 300' beyond. (Return to the main trail if you venture down here.) In another mile, you enter the forest and soon see Butler Creek Trail on your right. Continuing on the Beach Trail, it's just another half mile to the Ossagon Trail.

You'll cross Ossagon Creek before finding the sign for the trail, which climbs steeply up to Ossagon Prairie, the former site of a Yurok Indian village. The trail remains level briefly till it crosses Ossagon Creek via a bridge and about 20 stairs. From here you have just over a half mile of climbing to go before a nice downhill stretch to US 101. Use extreme caution as you turn onto US 101—there's a steep embankment from the trail to the highway, and you may find it best to dismount and walk your bike down onto the pavement. From here it's 6.2 miles, mostly downhill, back to the Prairie Creek Visitor Center.

RIDE 20 PRAIRIE CREEK REDWOODS STATE PARK
RIDE 21 LOST MAN CREEK TRAIL

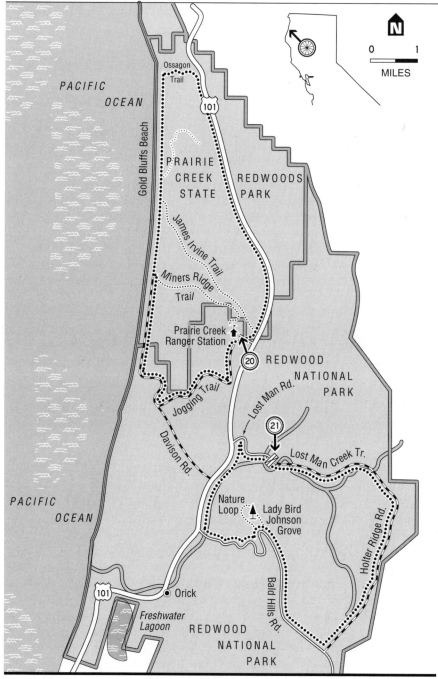

RIDE 21 *LOST MAN CREEK TRAIL*

This route through Redwood National Park can be ridden as a 19.4-mile loop or as an out-and-back ride that can be shortened by turning around at your leisure. The first half of the ride goes mostly uphill on a gravel road with a bed of pine needles to soften the ride. After you turn onto Bald Hills Road, your way is paved back to Lost Man Creek Road, which takes you back on gravel to the parking area.

This old road climbs up through redwood forest. You'll see the oldest, largest trees at the beginning of your ride, since the higher areas have been logged and the trees there are much smaller. In the first two miles, the road crosses Lost Man Creek twice. From the first two bridges, pause to enjoy the beautiful view of the stream. A third bridge crosses a small feeder stream from the north. Farther up, the forest is mixed with Douglas fir and redwoods. Other redwood-associated plants carpet the forest floor, such as sword and deer ferns, salal, redwood sorrel, thimbleberry, huckleberry, and salmonberry.

This trail is one of the least used in the entire park, and even in peak season, you may find more solitude here than on the other trails in the park that are open to mountain biking. On the way down Bald Hills Road, stop at the Lady Bird Johnson Grove to walk the 1.4-mile self-guiding nature trail. You can pick up a pamphlet that describes the walk at the beginning of the trail. If you're wondering why the grove is named after Lady Bird Johnson, it's because her strong support helped break a congressional deadlock over the establishment of this then-controversial national park. Bikes are prohibited on the nature trail but can be locked up in the nearby parking area.

General location: About 3 miles north of Orick and 2 miles south of the Prairie Creek Visitor Center.

Elevation change: Your route starts at about 150′ and climbs to 2,550′, losing about 500′ by the time it reaches Bald Hills Road.

Season: This park sees its heaviest use in the summer, when, ironically, thick fog blankets much of the coast. Fall usually brings drier, warmer weather and you're likelier to have the woods to yourself. If you pack raingear, you can ride many days during the wet but mild winter and spring months.

Services: All services are available in Orick, just three miles south of Lost Man Creek Road.

Hazards: The downhill on Bald Hills Road is very steep in some spots. Be sure to keep your speed under control.

Rescue index: In summer, you're likely to encounter people on the first 2 miles of this ride; otherwise, it's 2 miles from the trailhead to well-traveled US 101.

Land status: Redwood National Park.

Maps: See *Trails: Redwood National Park, California State Parks.* This small hiking map is available at visitor centers throughout the area for $1.

Finding the trail: Lost Man Creek Road is 2 miles south of the Prairie Creek Visitor Center and 3 miles north of Orick on US 101. Turn east at milepost 124.4; the entrance to the road is marked and has a small mountain bike sign. From here, it's 1.9 miles to the parking area.

Sources of additional information:

> Redwood National Park
> 1111 Second Street
> Crescent City, CA 95531
> (707) 464-6101 (24-hour information line)

For camping reservations write to:
> Ticketron
> P.O. Box 26430
> San Francisco, CA 94126

Notes on the trail: Ride through the turnstile and past the picnic area up Geneva Road. You'll cross the first bridge in less than a mile and the next one just 200′ beyond. The road begins to climb moderately, leveling out for short sections. After crossing the third bridge, the road begins to climb in earnest. At 1.5 miles, you're 100′ above Lost Man Creek; a mile later, you'll be 1,000′ above the trailhead. The road continues to climb until the 3.75-mile mark, where you reach a fork in the road. This is the eastern park boundary. To continue, turn right onto Holter Ridge Road, which follows the ridge and the park boundary to Bald Hills Road. This road eventually will climb to an elevation of 2,300′, but the rolling terrain helps you feel like you're not climbing the whole way.

Holter Ridge Road comes out onto Bald Hills Road about 6 miles from US 101. On the way down, detour over to the Lady Bird Johnson Grove on your right for an interesting short walk and a good chance to rest your braking hands. When you reach US 101, turn right and go the 2.2 miles to Lost Man Creek Road. Turn right again and ride the last couple of miles to the parking area. If you want to do this ride in reverse and just ride down to Lost Man Creek, you should avoid leaving your car on Bald Hills Road. Theft has been a problem in this area.

RIDE 22

ENDERTS BEACH / COASTAL TRAIL
(LAST CHANCE SECTION)

This ride is just over seven miles long one-way from Enderts Beach to US 101. You can ride it one-way by looping back on US 101 for a 12-mile ride, or you can pedal it as an out-and-back. The toughest section is in the first mile and a half. Most of the trail follows the old US 101 roadbed; however, where the highway has been washed away by the surf, the trail cuts inland and turns into a single-track that requires more handling ability. In just a half mile, the path leaves the old road and narrows. The steepest part of the whole trail is just beyond, where the trail gains 900′ in just over a mile. Take heart—the subsequent climbs are more gradual.

Variety is the joy of this ride. Near the beginning, you may choose to drop down onto Enderts Beach, where there are tidal pools and plenty of sandy beach to explore. As you ride, vistas of spectacular coastline alternate with the shadows of the stately redwoods.

Until 1935, US 101 was the main highway from Del Norte County to the rest of California. The road was closed to cars in 1970 because, as you can see, it's falling into the ocean; in many places, it's eroded to the point that there's not much left between the road and the surf below.

Just before you reach the five-mile mark, you'll pass several old highway markers, and just beyond these markers is a massive, 14-foot-wide redwood with a leather fern growing out of its side. The combination of coastal scrub and redwood forest habitat provides a diversity of vegetation including Douglas fir, alder, spruce, hemlock, coyote brush, sword fern, beach huckleberry, silk tassel, and salal, to name just a few.

General location: Two miles south of Crescent City on the west side of US 101.
Elevation change: Total elevation gain is 1,400′.
Season: Riding is possible throughout the year in this mild climate. The best months are September and October.
Services: From the trailhead it's only 4.7 miles to Crescent City, where you'll find all services and the Redwood National Park headquarters. Off-road camping is available on this trail at Nickels Beach, which is just under a mile round-trip hike or bike from the parking area. There are no services on site.
Hazards: Some portions of the trail are dangerous where the old road is falling into the sea. Always use caution around these areas, on bike or foot.

The trail has some steep, narrow sections. If you're not comfortable riding steep descents, get off and walk your bike.

If you stop to play on the beach, do not turn your back on the waves. Unusually large ones can catch you unaware and take you for an unplanned swim.

If you're going to be picked up at the end of this trail, the driver should wait at milepost 16 where there's a turnout. It's not quite a half mile south of the coastal trailhead, so be careful of traffic on US 101.

Rescue index: In summer, this is a popular trail so someone usually will come along soon. In winter, use slacks off but you're never more than 3.5 miles from either end of the trail.

Land status: Redwood National Park and Del Norte Coast Redwoods State Park.

Maps: You can pick up a small hiking map, *Trails: Redwood National Park, California State Parks,* at visitor centers throughout the area for one dollar.

Finding the trail: Two miles south of Crescent City on US 101, turn right onto Enderts Beach Road. Drive 2.5 miles to the parking area at the end of the road.

Sources of additional information:

Redwood National Park
1111 Second Street
Crescent City, CA 95531
(707) 464-6101

For camping reservations write to:
Ticketron
P.O. Box 26430
San Francisco, CA 94126

Notes on the trail: This ride has few intersections and is easy to follow. From the trailhead, a trail soon branches off to the right and leads down to Enderts Beach. If you'd like to explore this small beach, walk your bike down. Back on the main Coastal Trail, a second path to the right leads to Nickel Creek primitive campsite. After crossing over the creek, the Coastal Trail turns left, leaving the old roadbed.

The next 1.2 miles are the steepest section of your ride. If you're walking your bike up this part, don't worry—the rest will be easier. At the top of the steep stretch, the trail rejoins the old road and continues climbing to the first summit in about .3 miles. You then descend briefly and ride a generally level half mile until the second summit, followed by a nice downhill.

At 2.1 miles from the trailhead, you pass through a gate and enter the Del Norte Coast Redwoods State Park, gradually ascending for about a mile and a half. There's a small stream crossing; then the trail descends again to Damnation Creek at the 4.5-mile mark. If you don't want your feet to get wet, you'll have to cross the creek on a slippery log, so be careful!

From Damnation Creek to the intersection with the Damnation Trail, at 6 miles from your starting point, the trail remains mostly level with a few small climbs. The Damnation Trail is unmarked, but heads west-southwest from a big bend in the old road. The trail to the highway is 50' beyond. Continue on the old roadbed until the 7-mile mark, where a sign points uphill away from the old

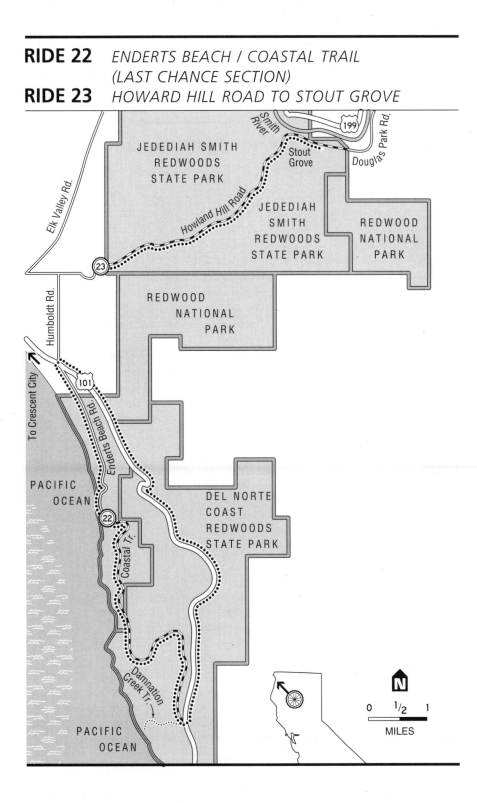

road. Cross over a small footbridge and you'll descend to US 101 in less than a quarter mile.

RIDE 23 *HOWLAND HILL ROAD TO STOUT GROVE*

This is a gorgeous 13-mile out-and-back ride, entirely on a small two-lane road that you'll share with others who want to see these spectacular redwoods. This road was once paved but is mostly gravel now; watch out for potholes. The second mile is the toughest as you climb up the ridge into the redwoods. After the summit, you cruise mostly downhill and over level terrain to Stout Grove.

Howland Hill Road originally was a stage road that ran from Crescent City north to Sailor Diggings and other mining camps in southwest Oregon. When it was built in 1858, it was known as the Crescent City and Yreka Turnpike. Today, this scenic route winds along the California coast and through a towering redwood forest.

Stout Grove is named for the family that donated the property to the state, not for the size of the trees, which indeed are stout. This grove is supposed to be the densest stand of redwoods on the California coast. The largest tree here measures 20′ in diameter and is 340′ tall. If you're a Steven Spielberg fan, you'll be interested to know that the Ewok scene in *Return of the Jedi* was filmed here.

General location: One mile from Crescent City.

Elevation change: The ride starts at 200′ and climbs to 530′ at Howland Summit. The trail then slowly drops back down to Stout Grove at 110′, for a total elevation gain of 750′.

Season: Enjoy this ride any time of year. Be prepared for fog and heavier use in summer, and for rain in winter and spring. Fall usually has the best weather.

Services: All services are located 1 mile north in Crescent City, including the Redwood National Park headquarters.

Hazards: The main hazard on this ride is vehicular traffic, mostly from slow-moving tourists who are enjoying the scenery. A few locals use the road as a shortcut to Crescent City, primarily in the winter when tourist traffic is light. Wear bright clothing so you can be seen in these dense woods.

Rescue index: Help should come along soon on this frequently traveled road.

Land status: Jedediah Smith Redwoods State Park.

Maps: A free map of this area is available at the Redwood National Park headquarters in Crescent City.

Finding the trail: On the southern edge of Crescent City, turn left onto Elk Valley Road. After 1 mile, turn right onto Howland Road. Park along the road here and begin riding. To avoid the tough climb into the park, you can drive up farther and park in a pulloff after Howland Summit.

Sources of additional information:

Redwood National Park
1111 Second Street
Crescent City, CA 95531
(707) 464-6101

For camping reservations write to:
Ticketron
P.O. Box 26430
San Francisco, CA 94126

Notes on the trail: From the beginning of Howland Hill Road it's 1 mile to the start of the uphill stretch. You'll pass a sign for Jedediah Smith Redwoods State Park a half mile past the start of the hill. The pavement ends .3 miles beyond the sign. You'll reach Howland Summit at the 2-mile mark; from here, the road is mostly level and flat. In a little less than 1 mile, you'll see the Memorial Metcalf Grove on your left. At 4.1 miles, the Boy Scout hiking trail leaves to your left. Further on, you'll cross a bridge over Mill Creek that provides a great view up-stream and down. At 6.2 miles from your starting point, the road to Stout Grove is on your left, and it's just a little farther to the parking area, where you can lock your bike. Enjoy the short walk through this majestic grove; you return to the bottom of Howland Hill Road the way you came.

Oroville

RIDE 24 *LAKE OROVILLE AQUEDUCT*

This pretty, seven-mile loop follows an aqueduct above Lake Oroville. It's a great ride for bikers of all abilities, covering mostly level terrain on a one-lane dirt road. A short climb and a nice downhill loops you back to the aqueduct road.

The only tricky section is the catwalk that runs alongside the aqueduct. First, you must shoulder your bike up a ladder about six-feet high; then, you cross a flat two-foot-wide walkway that's about six-feet long and drops into a ramp, down which you can walk your bike. If you can't lift your bike onto your shoulder and walk it up a ladder, bring a friend who can. Another option is to do this ride as an out-and-back.

The trail is a smooth gravel road that provides lesiurely views of the beautiful lake off to your left or the golden brown Sierra foothills off to your right. As you ride nearly five miles along the lakeshore, watch for osprey, blue heron, and bald eagle.

General location: Fourteen and a half miles east of Oroville.

Elevation change: The loop starts at 1,000' and drops to 900' before cresting at 1,300'. The trail goes back down to 900' and returns with a short climb to 1,000'.

Season: In summer, the road surface is hard and dry. It can get hot along the lake, where there isn't much shade. In fall, the changing leaves are beautiful and the temperature is perfect for riding. If the weather has been wet, count on getting a little muddy.

Services: There are no rest rooms or water on this ride. All services are available in Oroville.

Hazards: Use caution near the aqueduct, especially where the edge of it is level with the road surface. The aqueduct may look like fun to jump into, but it could be very difficult to get out of, or even deadly, when a large amount of water is flowing through.

Rescue index: Return to Forbestown Road for the closest assistance.

Land status: Lake Oroville State Recreation Area and county road.

Maps: USGS 7.5-minute series topographic map for Forbestown.

Finding the trail: Take CA 162 east out of Oroville for about 5 miles. Turn right onto Forbestown Road. In approximately 6.5 miles, turn left onto a wide, un-

This flume parallels the trail along Lake Oroville.

marked gravel road, and very soon you'll see another gravel road. Turn right and look for a large parking area and an orange gate across the road. Park and ride from here.

Sources of additional information:

Pullins Cyclery
801 Main Street
Chico, CA 95928
(916) 342-1055

RIDE 24 *LAKE OROVILLE AQUEDUCT*
RIDE 25 *FEATHER FALLS*

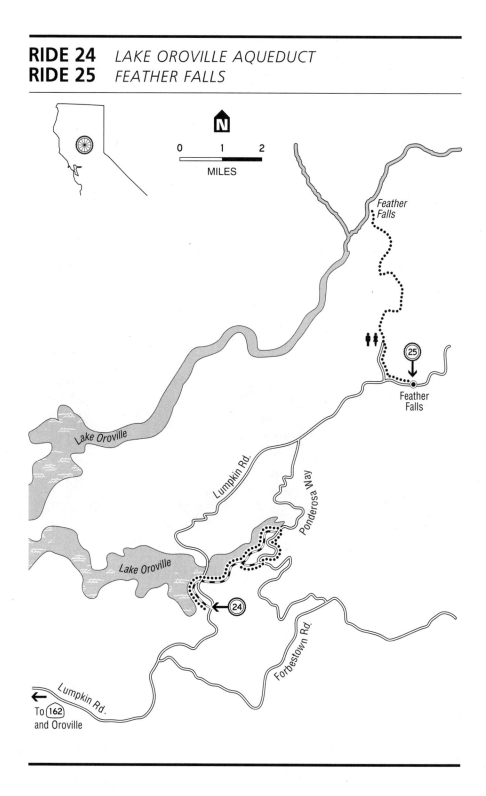

RIDE 25 *FEATHER FALLS*

You can extend this seven-mile out-and-back on dirt single-track by riding another four miles on pavement from the town of Feather Falls. Energetic beginners can do this ride but it has some tough sections. It was built as a hiking trail, so some areas are a little too steep and rocky for most mountain bikers. Near the end of the trail, it becomes almost a staircase; you may want to leave your bike here and walk the last section to the overlook.

Feather Falls is located in the foothills of the Sierra Nevada range. The town is at 3,000' and you can feel the altitude. The road to Feather Falls turns to dirt just outside of town, so it's quiet. Other than locals, not many people pass through.

The trail drops down through a forest with few open stretches until you get to the overlook. From there, the view of Feather Falls and south down the valley is breathtaking. There's no question that Feather Falls, the sixth-highest waterfall in the continental United States, is the highlight of this ride. If you want to see it at its peak, try March, April, or May. The falls run into the middle fork of the Feather River and on into Lake Oroville.

The pleasant town of Feather Falls also is worth visiting. Stop in at the historic post office, whose weathered barnboard exterior is worn smooth through years of use.

General location: Twenty-three miles east of Oroville.
Elevation change: The town of Feather Falls is at 2,950'. The trail drops to 1,600' and climbs briefly to 1,800' before dropping to 1,500' at the overlook.
Season: Late spring through late fall is the best time to ride this trail. In the spring, the trail may be a little muddy but the falls are spectacular, roaring off the side of the canyon 640' to the valley floor. In the summer, the falls taper off somewhat but attract many tourists; it's best to avoid weekends and holidays because traffic can become very heavy. Fall is great—the cooler temperatures are perfect for riding, the colors are beautiful, and most of the visitors are gone.
Services: The trailhead has toilets but no water or phone. There's a restaurant and a small store in Feather Falls. All other services are available in Oroville.
Hazards: This narrow trail can be very steep in certain areas, so keep your speed under control at all times.
Rescue index: The town of Feather Falls is the nearest source of assistance.
Land status: Plumas National Forest.
Maps: USGS 7.5-minute series topographic maps: Forbestown and Brush Creek.
Finding the trail: From Oroville, take CA 162 east for 7 miles. Turn right onto Forbestown Road. In 6 miles, turn left onto Lumpkin Road toward the town of Feather Falls, 11.5 miles ahead. I recommend that you park your car in town and

Splendid Feather Falls is located in the foothills of the Sierra Nevada range.

ride your bike to the trailhead. In the past, there have been some cars broken into at the trailhead.

Sources of additional information:

Pullins Cyclery
801 Main Street
Chico, CA 95928
(916) 342-1055

RIDE 26 *NORTH RIM TRAIL / BIDWELL PARK*

This is a seven-mile out-and-back jaunt. Mileage can be added by riding to the North Rim Trail through lower Bidwell Park, or by riding east from the trailhead, up through Bidwell Park along Big Chico Creek.

This ride is what you make of it. Taken at a slow pace, it can be moderate; if you push yourself, you can get a real workout. The road is rough, but neither steep nor narrow. The gravel road was carved out of basalt, a hard rock of volcanic origin, so expect bumpy riding. At the beginning, there's a single-track off to the left which is much smoother. After a tenth of a mile, it crosses over the road to the left-hand side and follows a fence. This route requires a bit more bike-handling skill because it's narrow. Use caution on the way down because it's easy to dent a rim on a rough road like this, as I found out.

The Rim Trail takes you up a ridge to an expansive view of the Central Valley. On most days, you can see the coastal hills to the west and the Sierra range to the east. To the south are Chico Canyon and Big Chico Creek. This is also a good spot for watching hawks and vultures ride the updrafts. In the valley, oaks grow in abundance and attract many other birds, specifically the acorn woodpecker.

General location: In the city of Chico.
Elevation change: The ride starts at 300′ and climbs to 1,200′ for a total elevation gain of 900′.
Season: This ride is accessible and fun to ride year-round. Early spring is beautiful—the hills are green and full of wildflowers. Summer temperatures can rise well into the 90s, so get an early start, take plenty of water, and pack a towel for a swim in Chico Creek. Fall brings ideal cycling weather with cool, sunny days, and vivid fall colors as the leaves on the huge white oaks and sycamores turn in October and November.
Services: All services, including several bike shops, are available in Chico.
Hazards: The rough road can be tough on you and your bike. It's easy to dent a rim if your air pressure is low, and the bumpiness will rattle off anything that

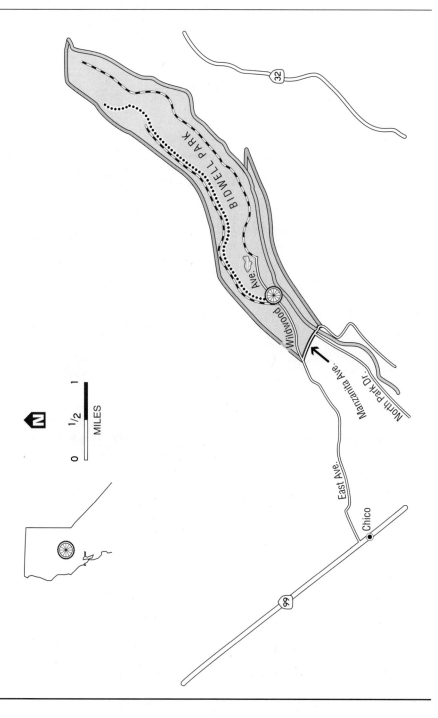

Easy pedaling along the Lake Oroville Reservoir.

is loose. As always, check out your machine ahead of time, and be sure to carry a tool kit.

The smoother single-track alternative to the rough main trail runs alongside a barbed-wire fence that may make some riders nervous.

Rescue index: Return to the trailhead for assistance.

Land status: Chico city park.

Maps: A city map of Chico will show the roads leading to this ride. If you'd like more detail, use the USGS 7.5-minute quad for Richardson Springs.

Finding the trail: There are several ways to get to Bidwell Park. I recommend that you start in downtown Chico and ride northeast on South Park Drive, then continue onto the North Rim Trail. This route is especially fun before 11 A.M.

because the park is closed to motor vehicles. The road travels along Chico Creek and is lined with oaks and green meadows. At the intersection with Manzanita Avenue, turn left. The next street to your right is Wildwood. Turn right on Wildwood, and in 1 mile you'll see a sign for the North Rim Trail on the left. Park your car in the pulloff on either side of the street where the trail begins.

Sources of additional information:

Pullins Cyclery
801 Main Street
Chico, CA 95928
(916) 342-1055

Redding

RIDE 27 *CLIKAPUDI CREEK TRAIL*

A fun eight-mile loop, this ride is a single-track dirt trail, with a short section of dirt road. The loop is suitable for the novice rider and has some tricky turns that will challenge even the experienced mountain biker. The first mile and a half is a gentle grade but once you cross the paved road, the hill steepens and presents a series of switchbacks with tight corners that are hard to negotiate. Beyond this short steep section, there's a smooth downhill. The last four miles are mostly flat with some small uphills.

Most of the route follows a hiking path. About halfway along, the trail turns into a gravel road for about a half mile. The second half of the ride has a few turns that are sometimes difficult because they are followed by short, steep uphills. Overall, the trail is well maintained and easy to ride.

The large recreation area of Shasta Lake brings many people to this area. You'll have many views of the man-made lake as you ride along Clikapudi Bay. The water level of this reservoir fluctuates towards the low side, so there's often a sizable gap between the shoreline and the vegetation line. The trail takes you through oak, madrone, Douglas fir, as well as poison oak; be careful if you wander off the trail. Take the time to stop and look around. You should see woodpeckers, chickadees, robins, blue herons, grouse, quail, ospreys, and many other birds. You may also see squirrels and deer.

This trail also passes through an area rich with Wintu Indian history. The name "Clikapudi" comes from a Wintu word meaning "to kill," and refers to a battle between the Wintu and local traders. About halfway through the ride, you'll see a large fenced area where excavations of a Wintu village site are visible. Please do not disturb this area.

General location: About 15 miles northeast of Redding.
Elevation change: The trail starts at 1,100′ and climbs to 1,300′ before gently rolling back to 1,100′.
Season: The best times of year to ride this trail are in fall or spring, and perhaps a few days in winter, as long as there is no snow on the ground. Fall riding is the most pleasant because the ground is dry and hard, giving you good traction, and there are fewer people on the trails. Summer riding is problematic in this very

The trails around Shasta Lake are well maintained and in fall are not heavily traveled.

popular area; if you do ride in the summer, prepare yourself to stop often, or try to get an early start.

Services: There are rest rooms and water at the Jones Valley boat ramp. About 2 miles down the road towards Redding, there's a small store on the left that's a convenient spot for a cold drink. All services are available in Redding.

Hazards: If you plan to ride on a midsummer weekend, be very careful of pedestrians on this multi-use trail. Be especially careful at the one intersection with a paved road, and look both ways when crossing.

Poison oak can be a problem but only if you wander off the trail.

Rescue index: The availability of help depends on the time of year. When the trails aren't busy, the best policy is to ride with a friend.

Land status: Shasta-Trinity National Forest.

Maps: There are three good maps for this area. The Shasta-Trinity National Forest map gives you a nice overview. If you'd like more detail, the ranger station in Redding has a free 3-page photocopy of several hiking routes around Shasta Lake. Three of the trails described in that handout are in this book; the others are not recommended for mountain biking. The USGS topographic map for Bella Vista (7.5-minute series) does not show the trail but is useful for figuring out elevation changes in this region.

Finding the trail: The trail begins at the southwest corner of the parking lot for the Jones Valley boat ramp, approximately 15 miles northeast of Redding. Follow signs to Jones Valley from I-5 and park your car anywhere in the huge lot.

Sources of additional information:

> Chain Gang Bike Shop
> 2665 Park Marina Drive
> Redding, CA 96001
> (916) 243-7101

> Shasta Lake Ranger District
> Shasta-Trinity National Forest
> 6543 Holiday Drive
> Redding, CA 96003
> (916) 275-1587

Notes on the trail: Look for the hiker and Clikapudi Trail signs in the southwest corner of the parking lot. For the first mile, the trail runs along the lake. Watch closely for an intersection where the trail either goes straight or turns sharply up a switchback to the left. If you go straight, you'll be on the Clikapudi Spur Trail, a short out-and-back to the lower Jones Valley campground. Take a sharp left onto the main trail that takes you up to the paved road. Turn right, and you'll see another hiker sign just a few yards down the road on the left. Continue on this trail up the switchbacks and down the other side of the hill along Clikapudi Creek. The next intersection is in a large open area where an access road has been built to the archeological sites. Stay left here, and follow the road until it crosses a small creek. The single-track continues straight here and follows Clikapudi Bay out to Shasta Lake and back to the boat ramp parking lot.

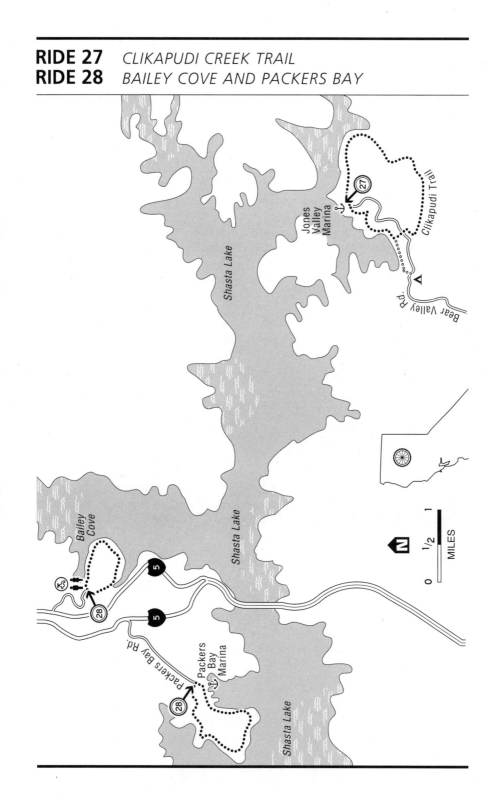

RIDE 28 *BAILEY COVE AND PACKERS BAY*

These two, short single-track loops can be combined to give you more exercise. Since bicycles are prohibited on I-5, you'll have to drive your car between the two. If you're driving from Redding, it's easiest to do the Bailey Cove loop first because the freeway is divided. Then it's a short drive north before you can turn back south to do the Packers Bay loop.

The Bailey Cove Trail is 2.9 miles long. Packers Bay has four short trails; I like to combine the Waters Gulch Trail (3.2 miles) and the Fish Loop Trail (0.5 miles). None of these trails is very difficult but there are short sections, including tricky curves over small bridges, that some riders may have to walk. Both rides have great views of Shasta Lake and the surrounding hills. The trails go through mixed woods of oak, Douglas fir, madrone, and pine, and are especially nice in the fall when the deciduous trees change colors and drop their leaves.

Most people come to this area to use Shasta Lake, which also attracts plenty of birds. Watch for gulls, Canada geese, ospreys, ducks, and blue herons. The Bailey Cove loop circles a hill that clearly demonstrates how the sun affects tree growth. The south side of the hill is hot and arid, and here you'll see manzanita and knobcone pines. On the north side of the hill, these trees give way to pines and oaks and then to a thick forest of Douglas fir.

General location: Both loops are about 16 miles north of Redding on opposite sides of I-5.

Elevation change: The overall change in elevation is minimal on either of these rides. On the Packers Bay loop, you start at 1,100' and climb to 1,300'. At Bailey Cove, the elevation is 1,150' and doesn't vary much along the loop.

Season: Spring is always a fun time of year to dust off the bike, and these are scenic short rides to begin with. Shasta Lake should be full with spring runoff. Summer weather is fine up here, but avoid the weekend and holiday crowds. Fall is ideal: most everyone has gone home, the weather's still nice, and the trails are empty. All the oak leaves have fallen and it's a blast to ride through them. In November, the Forest Service closes the Bailey Cove area but you may still walk or ride in. The rest rooms are closed and the water is turned off but there is a pay phone. Winter riding is possible—but chilly—as long as there's no snow on the ground.

Services: Both areas have water, rest rooms, and a phone, although the Forest Service shuts down all but the phones at Bailey Cove and Packers Bay in November. All other services can be found in Redding.

Hazards: Watch for other people using the trail, especially on summer weekends.

Rescue index: Both areas are busy in the summer, so help is usually nearby. If

Packers Pay and Bailey Cove have great single-track trails.

you plan on riding in the off-season, be sure to let someone know where you're going. A phone is always within 2 miles at most and is located by the rest rooms.
Land status: Shasta-Trinity National Forest.
Maps: For an overview of the region, see the Shasta-Trinity National Forest map. For more detail, see the free hiking map of Shasta Lake, available at the ranger station in Redding. For topographic information, refer to the USGS 15-minute quad for Lamoine.
Finding the trail: The Bailey Cove loop is about 16 miles north of Redding. Take the O'Brien exit off of I-5, turn right, and follow the sign for the boat ramp area. For Packers Bay (after riding Bailey Cove), get back onto I-5 going south and take the exit for Packers Bay Road. There are large parking lots at each trailhead, and the trails are clearly marked.

Sources of additional information:

Chain Gang Bike Shop
2665 Park Marina Drive
Redding, CA 96001
(916) 243-7101

Shasta Lake Ranger District
Shasta-Trinity National Forest
6543 Holiday Drive
Redding, CA 96003
(916) 275-1587

Notes on the trail: Both of these rides are easy single-tracks with very clear routes. Just remember that you are sharing the trail with hikers, so be extra careful on blind curves. Both rides have short sections that you might prefer to walk, but I leave that to your skill and judgment.

RIDE 29 *BOULDER CREEK LOOP*

This 8.5-mile loop follows a wide path through the hills above Clear Creek and the Whiskeytown Dam. The first two miles climb a tough hill that many riders have been known to walk. Not to worry—you'll be rewarded by a mostly downhill ride the rest of the way. There are several exciting creek crossings, but these are small enough for the more timid rider to easily get across with dry feet.

Most of this loop covers wide gravel roads. As you start down Boulder Creek, the trail narrows with a few tricky eroded spots. There are some little gullies and rocky sections where you may need to slow down in order to ensure a trouble-free ride.

At the summit, a spectacular view is gratification for your rigorous climb through pine, maple, oak, and madrone. To the north is the Clear Creek Valley and to the south are the ridges leading up to Shasta Bally (6,209 feet). After two more short climbs, the trail drops down into the Boulder Creek Valley. Boulder Creek runs year-round off the slopes of Shasta Bally, and its five crossings make for a cool and delightful summertime ride.

Despite the beauty of the trees and mountains, the highlight of this ride may be an encounter with one of the many animals that live in these woods. Take the time to observe and you may see nuthatches, jays, woodpeckers, grouse, quail, flycatchers, or owls, as well as squirrels, deer, and an occasional black bear. A story is told locally about a cyclist who once ran right into a bear on this very trail, so watch your speed!

General location: Fifteen miles west of Redding on CA 299.
Elevation change: Total elevation gain and loss is 1,200'.
Season: This loop is enjoyable any time of the year. The spring wildflowers only last a few weeks but are lovely. Summer riding here is great because much of the trail is in the shade. Fall offers spectacular colors and adds a new dimension to the ride when you cannot see the ground because of the fallen leaves. Winter

RIDE 29 *BOULDER CREEK LOOP*

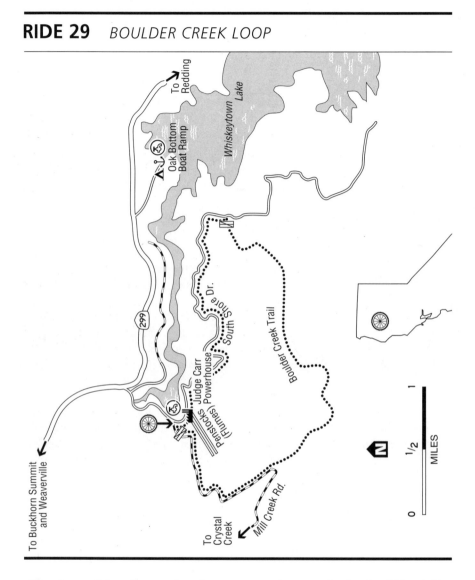

riding is possible as long as there is no snow on the ground—but it will be chilly, so wear something warm.

Services: You'll find rest rooms and water at the Carr Powerhouse picnic area. Snacks and beverages are sold at the Whiskeytown Store just 4.5 miles down the road towards Redding. (Watch for signs; it's off the main road.) Camping is available at several campgrounds around the lake. Stop in at the park headquarters for more information and a free map.

The intersection of Boulder Creek Trail and Mill Creek Road is a scenic place to stop and catch your breath.

Hazards: Rocky areas on the single-track portion of the trail become even trickier in the fall when leaves cover the rocks.

Rescue index: You'll never be farther than 4.2 miles from your car. A pay phone is available at the Whiskeytown Store.

Land status: Whiskeytown-Shasta-Trinity National Recreation Area.

Maps: The free map offered at the park headquarters is a nice general guide for this area. For more detail, get the USGS topographic maps for French Gulch and Whiskeytown (7.5-minute series).

Finding the trail: Take CA 299 west from Redding for approximately 15 miles to the west end of Whiskeytown Lake. Watch for the sign to the Judge Francis Carr Powerhouse. On your way into the parking area, look for a gravel jeep road on the right to Crystal Creek. Park your car at the picnic area and backtrack out the way you came in. Turn left onto Crystal Springs Road.

Sources of additional information:

Chain Gang Bike Shop
2665 Park Marina Drive
Redding, CA 96001
(916) 243-7101

Whiskeytown Unit
Whiskeytown-Shasta-Trinity National Recreation Area
P.O. Box 188
Whiskeytown, CA 96095-0188

Notes on the trail: As you turn left onto a jeep road toward Crystal Springs, the pavement ends. At the Y-intersection veer right (the left fork leads to the penstocks). You may find a green gate blocking the road, which is closed in fall and winter for erosion control. Go around the gate if it's closed. The next 2 miles are uphill on a wide dirt and gravel road. At the intersection of Boulder Creek Trail and Mill Creek Road, continue straight ahead. From this point, the trail narrows into single-track for about 3 miles. At the bottom of the hill, go around another gate and turn left onto South Shore Drive, which leads back to the Carr Powerhouse parking area.

RIDE 30 *MOUNT SHASTA MINE LOOP*

Try this very easy 3.5-mile loop through a once-bustling mining area. The single-track trail is smooth and level. Occasionally, you may find a tree blocking the road; if you can't move it, you may have to climb over it or go around to continue. As you ride, keep your eyes open for a few reminders of past dreams, such as old mine shafts cut out of the rock. Not far down the trail are the remains of Mount Shasta Mine. There isn't much left to see other than a hole in the ground with a chain-link fence around it. This mine was the principal producer of gold ore in the Shasta mining district and operated from 1897 to 1905, peaking in 1899. The entire Whiskeytown region was the site of a large gold rush in 1848. For more information, stop in at Old Shasta, which was the center of gold-mining activity and is now a historic landmark.

General location: Fifteen miles west of Redding on CA 299.
Elevation change: The ride starts at 1,140' and the highest point is 1,200'.
Season: Spring through late fall are excellent times to do this ride; however it's very accessible from Redding year-round, as long as there is no snow on the ground.

RIDE 30   *MOUNT SHASTA MINE LOOP*

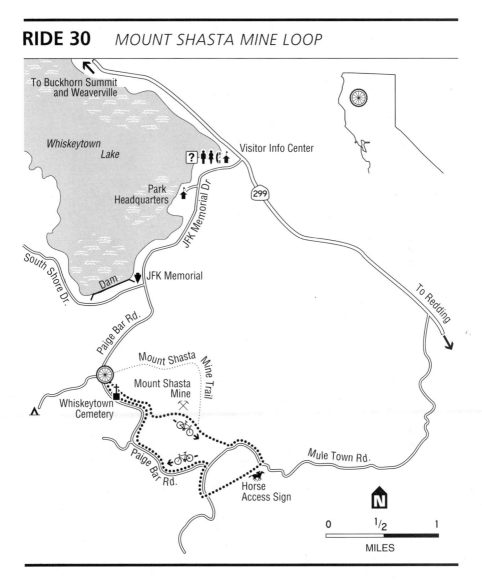

Services: Water, phones, and rest rooms are available at the Visitor Center. All other services are available in Redding.

Hazards: Watch for cars when going from the trail onto roads, and be prepared to encounter horses on the single-track.

Rescue index: Help is available at the park headquarters.

Land status: The Whiskeytown unit of the Whiskeytown-Shasta-Trinity National Recreation Area.

Stop to peek into the old Shasta Mine shaft.

Maps: The free park map available at the Visitor Center is a nice general guide for this area. For more detail, check the USGS topographic map for Igo (7.5-minute series).

Finding the trail: From Redding, take CA 299 west for approximately 8 miles. Turn left toward the Visitor Center and veer left onto Paige Bar Road. In 1.2 miles, you'll see a large gravel area on the left, which is the trailhead for the Mount Shasta Mine loop. Park your car here. One trail goes directly east and uphill. The trail described here starts in the southeast corner of the parking lot and is fairly level.

Sources of additional information:

Chain Gang Bike Shop
2665 Park Marina Drive
Redding, CA 96001
(916) 243-7101

Whiskeytown Unit
Whiskeytown-Shasta-Trinity National Recreation Area
P.O. Box 188
Whiskeytown, CA 96095-0188

Notes on the trail: Follow the Mount Shasta Mine Trail past the mine until you come out on Mule Town Road. Turn left and ride for approximately a half mile. Make the next right onto a single-track trail with a small horse sign, showing that it is open to equestrians. Turn right, back onto Mule Town Road, and then take the next left onto Paige Bar Road. When you come to a Y-intersection, keep right and follow Paige Bar Road back to the parking area.

Mount Shasta

RIDE 31 *SISKIYOU LAKE LOOP*

This is a very easy 10.5-mile loop ride, though sometimes fording the headwaters of the Sacramento River can be difficult. You must walk your bike through the river as you balance on a series of rocks, and the best rocks to cross on are not obvious. The ideal place to cross will probably change from one winter flood to the next. We had the best luck downstream from where the road once crossed the stream. During spring runoff plan on getting your feet wet.

If you begin in the town of Mount Shasta, your loop mileage will be 14.5. There's about a two-mile stretch of pavement before you turn right onto the dirt surface of North Shore Road. After crossing the river and scrambling over some rocks, there's just a brief section of dirt road before the pavement resumes.

In spring, look for wildflowers along the way. As summer moves across the landscape, watch for a variety of wildlife including juncos, sparrows, woodpeckers, and deer. Fall brings small splashes of color in a predominantly pine forest. Throughout all the seasons, the lofty summit of Mount Shasta remains the scenic highlight of the ride once you're out of the trees, although you'll also catch views of Siskiyou Lake through the trees. But stream crossing is potentially the most exciting part of the ride—imagine telling your friends that you walked your bike across the Sacramento River.

General location: Two miles southwest of the town of Mount Shasta.
Elevation change: The town of Mount Shasta is at 3,400′ and the ride never gains or drops more than 80′ throughout.
Season: The best time to ride in this area is late spring to early fall. Depending on the snowpack, the Sacramento might be too full and fast to wade through in the spring, but by summer, the river has lowered and a dip feels great.
Services: You'll need to fill your water bottles in town. There's also water on the far side of the lake at the Siskiyou Lake Campground. All other services are available in the town of Mount Shasta.
Hazards: Although this is a short, easy ride, it's generally sound practice to let others know where you are going and how long you expect to be gone. Be prepared for quick drops in temperature at this high elevation.

The crossing of the Sacramento River is the most difficult obstacle on this ride

When you ride around Siskiyou Lake you'll have great views of Mount Shasta.

and that will vary according to the water level. Shortly after the stream crossing, you return to the pavement, so watch for motorists.

Rescue index: This ride is very close to the town of Mount Shasta but there is also Siskiyou Lake Campground and several residences along either end of the ride.

Land status: Shasta-Trinity National Forest.

Maps: Shasta-Trinity National Forest maps are available at ranger stations throughout this area for $2.

Finding the trail: You can start this ride in town or drive out to North Shore Road. From downtown Mount Shasta, take Lake Street west out of town and over I-5. At the T-intersection, turn left onto Old Stage Road. From here, Siskiyou Lake is 3 miles. The road soon splits; veer right onto Barr Road. In less than a mile, turn right onto North Shore Road, which begins as a paved road but soon turns to dirt. If you chose to drive from town, park your car on North Shore Road in the pulloff where the pavement turns to dirt.

Sources of additional information:

The Fifth Season
426 North Mount Shasta Boulevard
Mount Shasta, CA 96067
(916) 926-3606

Mount Shasta Ranger District
Shasta-Trinity National Forest
204 West Alma
Mount Shasta, CA 96067

Notes on the trail: This ride follows the north shore of Siskiyou Lake and goes up along the Sacramento River. The first intersection is signed. To the right is Dead End Road; continue on the road to the left. Immediately after this intersection is a bridge over the Deer River, and beyond it is another stream crossing. Although there's no bridge at the second crossing, the creek is small. After you cross the creek, begin watching for a road to the left that has been blocked by a pile of dirt. Turn left onto this road to cross the Sacramento River. (If you miss this turn, the road will follow the river but eventually gets too rough to ride. Just backtrack and look for the blocked turn, now on your right.)

The crossing of the Sacramento may take some research the first time. It can be done keeping your feet dry or even more easily if you don't mind wet shoes, but watch out for slippery rocks. Pick up the road on the other side of the river. Turn left in a tenth of a mile where the gravel road intersects with the pavement. This is Barr Road, which follows the south shore of the lake, back to the intersection with North Shore Road.

RIDE 31 *SISKIYOU LAKE LOOP*
RIDE 32 *McCLOUD RAILROAD GRADE*

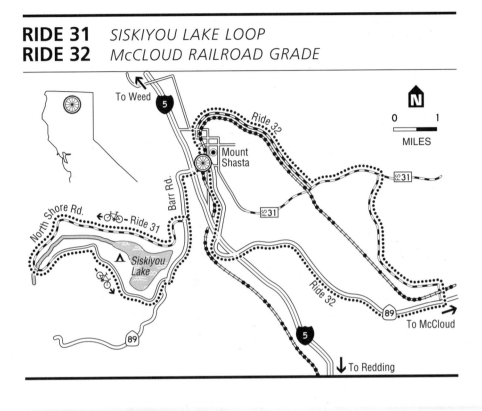

RIDE 32 *McCLOUD RAILROAD GRADE*

This approximately 17-mile ride can be done as a loop or as a long downhill if someone gives you a ride up to Ski Park Highway. If you start your ride in town, the first part of the ride is level until you turn onto CA 89. From here, the road climbs all the way to the turnoff onto Ski Park Highway. The grade is never steeper than 6 percent and it's worthwhile for the long dirt downhill along the railroad tracks. These first eight miles are paved until you turn off Ski Park Highway onto Forest Service Road 40N24, a dirt road in good condition because it's often used by loggers. A half-mile section, on FS 31 is the roughest section of the whole ride; be careful of the large potholes.

This route climbs up the south side of Mount Shasta, then traverses around to the west side of the mountain. As you ride through the trees, spectacular views will appear of the valley and the mountain peak. Below you'll see beautiful Siskiyou Lake and the headwaters of the Sacramento River. Watch carefully and you

Black Butte can be seen from many of the Mount Shasta area rides.

may observe a variety of juncos, flickers, sparrows, nuthatches, jays, and deer. You also may see some lumber from McCloud go rolling past on the railroad, which is still in use today.

General location: In and near the town of Mount Shasta.
Elevation change: The town of Mount Shasta is at 3,400′. CA 89 climbs to 4,478′ before a long gentle downhill takes you back to town with one short climb of 120′. Total elevation gain and loss is 1,198′.
Season: Late spring through late fall. As with all high-elevation riding, be prepared for extreme temperature changes.
Services: All services are available in the town of Mount Shasta. For camping information, stop by the ranger station located at 204 West Alma in Mount Shasta.
Hazards: The most dangerous section of this ride is the turn onto CA 89. Be aware of traffic merging from I-5 onto CA 89. Once you've turned off of CA 89, the dirt road is generally smooth except for a half-mile section of potholes on FS 31.
Rescue index: Once you turn onto the dirt road, you won't see much traffic. Sometimes this area is open to woodcutters, but don't count on them to find you if you take a spill. Always be sure to let people know where you are going and when you plan on returning if you ride alone. To shorten the ride stay on FS 31, which will bring you back to town sooner than continuing on the railroad grade.
Land status: Shasta-Trinity National Forest.
Maps: The Shasta-Trinity National Forest Service map shows all of the roads

on this ride and is available for $2 at ranger stations throughout this area. For more detail, use the USGS topographic maps for the town of Mount Shasta and for McCloud (7.5-minute series).

Finding the trail: From downtown Mount Shasta, take Mount Shasta Boulevard south out of town and follow signs for CA 89 to McCloud. If you park your car in town, be careful to leave it where you won't get a parking ticket.

Sources of additional information:

> The Fifth Season
> 426 North Mount Shasta Boulevard
> Mount Shasta, CA 96067
> (916) 926-3606

> Mount Shasta Ranger District
> Shasta-Trinity National Forest
> 204 West Alma
> Mount Shasta, CA 96067
> (916) 926-4511

Notes on the trail: From CA 89 towards McCloud, turn left onto Ski Park Highway. In less than a mile, turn left just beyond the railroad tracks onto FS 40N24, which parallels the tracks for 3 miles. At the 1.5-mile mark, a large dirt road intersects, but you continue straight. At the 3-mile mark, the road veers right to the north, and climbs for about a mile through some clearcut areas which allow views of Mount Shasta and the valley below. In a little over 4 miles, turn left at the T-intersection onto FS 31. In a half mile, turn right before you cross the railroad tracks. This one-lane dirt road parallels the tracks all the way until it intersects with the paved Everett Memorial Highway.

In a half mile, there's a small stream crossing, and just beyond is a mobile home on the right and a water tower on the left. You'll see a road that crosses the tracks here. If you'd like to shorten your ride, cross the tracks and drop down the hill into the town of Mount Shasta. For more smooth downhill dirt riding, continue on the right side of the tracks and turn left once you intersect with the pavement. This is the Everett Memorial Highway, which turns into Washington Street and then intersects with Mount Shasta Boulevard, in downtown Mount Shasta.

RIDE 33 *RIDE AROUND MOUNT SHASTA (RAMS)*

This 63-mile loop around Mount Shasta, an isolated volcanic cone, is not recommended for those who are not in great shape. However, if you feel ready to tackle this ride, start early and travel prepared. Depending on the season, it could

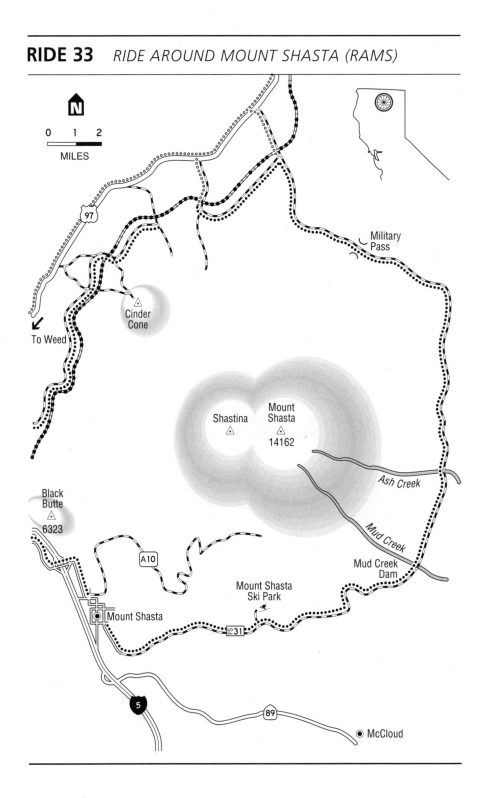

be cold in the morning and hot at midday, so you'll need to dress appropriately. You'll also need to carry enough food and water for a long ride, as well as tools to cover your mechanical needs. If you carry tools, you probably won't need them; if you don't have them, it's a long walk home.

This ride has a variety of surface conditions, including large gravel, sand, and washboard bumps. The ride starts out on pavement which soon turns to dirt, and the first half of the ride combines dirt and gravel roads. The short two-mile section climbing up and over Military Pass can be sandy in the dry season. At about the 41-mile mark, the maintained road disappears and you must ride alongside the railroad tracks on a very rough and slow section of large gravel. Beyond this is another short stretch of dirt, followed by pavement for the last few miles back to the town of Mount Shasta.

You'll experience a broad range of scenery on this ride. Around the eastern slopes of Mount Shasta, there are many small streams, Ash Creek being one of the largest. Beyond, you'll pedal through high desert filled with sage and juniper. Desolate lava flows from the volcano's more active past characterize the northwestern section. The first highlight is Mud Creek Dam at mile 16, the site of a large mudflow which occurred in the 1960s. It came roaring down the mountain towards McCloud but stopped short of the town.

General location: Mount Shasta.

Elevation change: Your route includes one long climb, but after that you'll encounter only rolling terrain. Total gain and loss in elevation is approximately 3,500′.

Season: This route usually is rideable from late spring through late fall. The road can be a little muddy in the spring but the sandy section over Military Pass is usually firm then, and the wildflowers can be spectacular. The midsummer months are the best because the long days give you more time to enjoy the ride. Be careful in September and October because it is deer season; wear bright clothing! As winter gets near, be prepared for sudden weather changes and cold temperatures. Dress in layers year-round, since temperatures can fluctuate widely at higher elevations, even in summer.

Services: The town of Mount Shasta is your only source of services. Be sure to take plenty of food and water with you on this ride. Clean water will not be available on the trail, so you'll need to carry either a purifier or purification tablets. For any bicycle needs or for further information about this ride, stop by the Fifth Season in the town of Mount Shasta.

Hazards: I cannot stress enough the need to carry sufficient water. Please carry at least 3 quarts and refill at Ash Creek (mile 19), your last reliable source of water. The Creek's purity is not reliable, however, so use purification tablets or a water filter.

Logging trucks may be on some of these roads; when you hear one coming, give it plenty of space because the driver may not expect a mountain biker.

The climb up Military Pass may be sandy, resulting in slow riding or walking, and overall frustration. Be patient, however; this section is only about 2 miles long. Farther on are nearly 15 miles of rough riding along the railroad tracks and an optional crossing of a trestle that may be hazardous since the tracks are still in use. As always, but especially on a long ride, be sure your machine is in good working order, and carry tools and spare parts with you.

Rescue index: It's possible to be 30 miles from help on this ride, so your safest bet is to go with a friend and leave word behind about where you are going and when you expect to return.

Land status: Shasta-Trinity National Forest and railroad access.

Maps: The Shasta-Trinity National Forest map (available at ranger stations throughout the area for $2) is good but if you'd like more detail, the USGS 7.5-minute series quads are Mount Shasta, Hotlum, McCloud, and Ash Creek Butte.

Finding the trail: Park your car in downtown Mount Shasta in any area that doesn't have a time limit. Ride south on Mount Shasta Boulevard.

Sources of additional information:

The Fifth Season
426 North Mount Shasta Boulevard
Mount Shasta, CA 96067
(916) 926-3606

Mount Shasta Ranger District
Shasta-Trinity National Forest
204 West Alma
Mount Shasta, CA 96067

Notes on the trail: From downtown Mount Shasta, ride south on Mount Shasta Boulevard. Turn left onto Old McCloud Road and climb until you reach Ski Park Highway at mile 7. Turn left onto Ski Park Highway and after approximately a quarter mile, the paved road gradually turns left, but you want to continue straight onto a dirt road. You'll climb for 4 or 5 miles, passing springs along the road at mile 14. You'll then descend for 2 miles to Mud Creek Dam. After a 3-mile climb, the ride levels off for about 6 miles.

Ash Creek at mile 19 is the only major stream crossing. Fill your water bottles here, because your next challenge is climbing Military Pass. After a gradual climb to the summit, and 3 miles beyond the downhill, you'll reach an intersection. At this intersection (mile 36), take a left-hand turn onto Andesite Road. Climb for one mile and make the first right at the Y-intersection. Enjoy this fun downhill section with banked curves.

Stay on the main road until you intersect with the railroad tracks at mile 41. At this point, you may continue straight out to US 97, where a left turn will take you into the town of Weed. US 97 doesn't make for a shorter ride but it is a smoother ride, since it avoids the rough gravel along the railroad tracks and the dangerous trestle crossing.

If you follow the railroad tracks, you'll be on rough gravel because there's no established road. Just north of Hotlum at mile 46, as you're riding along the south side of the train tracks, you'll come to a railroad trestle. You have the option to dash across the trestle or climb down into the valley and back out again. Ride on the north side until you get to the Black Butte siding yard. The large black water tank here is a good landmark. Cross the tracks at the water tank and ride on the southeast side until you see a dirt road on the left. Then take the first right and follow this major dirt road back to the pavement. The pavement runs on the northwest side of Black Butte. Turn left and continue to Interstate 5, which you'll ride under before turning left again onto Summit Drive. Head south to Abrams Lake Road and turn left back across I-5. Turn right on Spring Hill Drive and follow it to Mount Shasta Boulevard. Turn left and follow this back into the town of Mount Shasta.

Thanks to Max Tenscher, who gave me this information, and to Leif Voeltz of the Fifth Season, who introduced me to Max.

Sacramento

RIDE 34 *LATROBE ROAD*

This is a fun, mellow 12.6-mile out-and-back in the country, away from the crowds of Sacramento but without the drive to the mountains. There isn't much change in elevation, and the gravel road surface is smooth, so novices will enjoy this ride.

The quiet, tranquil, open route winds close to the Sierra foothills, where the terrain is more rolling than in the flat Central Valley. This area is used mostly for grazing, so cattle are your companions and the picturesque farmhouses are several miles apart. Once in a while, you'll see a hawk hovering over the fields, looking for a meal.

General location: Thirty-five miles east of Sacramento, just west of the town of Latrobe.

Elevation change: The ride begins at 800', then Latrobe Road drops down to 200' on the Consumnes River.

Season: This road is beautiful year-round, but it can get muddy if there's been much rain. Spring here is glorious: the hills still are green and the wildflowers are showing their colors. As summer moves in, the hills quickly change to golden brown. Midsummer temperatures get very hot and there's little shade, so carry plenty of water. Fall's perfectly sunny, cool days make for ideal riding. In winter, this road remains accessible when many favorite upland rides are covered in snow.

Services: All services are available in Sacramento. There are no public facilities on the route itself.

Hazards: Unless a cow gets loose, the only thing to look out for is an occasional motorized vehicle.

Rescue index: Local cars pass about every half hour. If you need roadside help, these will be your closest source, unless a farmhouse is in view.

Land status: County roads.

Maps: Any reasonably detailed street map of the Sacramento area should include these roads. For more detail, refer to the USGS 7.5-minute quadrants for Folsom SE and Latrobe.

Finding the trail: From Sacramento, take US 50 east to the El Dorado Hills/ Latrobe exit. Go south on Latrobe Road 8.5 miles. Turn right at South Shingle

RIDE 34 *LATROBE ROAD*

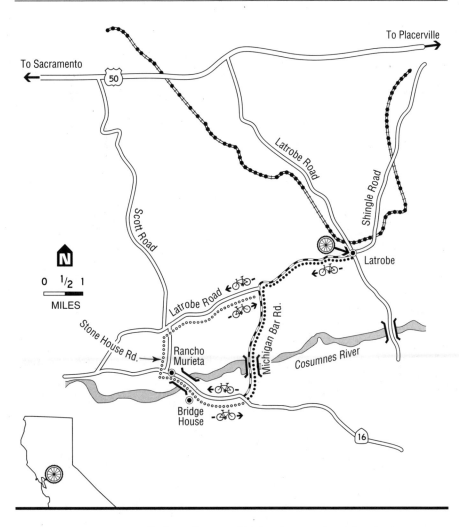

Road. At the top of the hill, Miller's Hill School is on the right. Park your car here. The dirt road begins soon after the school.

Sources of additional information:

Adventure Mountain Bikes
11383 Pyrites Way
Rancho Cordova, CA 95670
(916) 638-8575

Latrobe Road goes through some peaceful farm country.

Notes on the trail: From Miller's Hill School, go west on South Shingle Road. In approximately three miles, turn left onto unmarked Michigan Bar Road, which is the first road you'll see. Ride on Michigan Bar Road until you reach the bridge over the Cosumnes River. Stop here and return the way you came.

For a longer ride, do not turn onto Michigan Bar Road. Instead, continue straight on South Shingle Road to Stone House Road and turn left. When you intersect with a large, busy road (CA 16), turn left. Watch for Michigan Bar Road on your left. Turn left onto Michigan Bar Road and follow it back to Latrobe Road, where you'll turn right and return to Miller's Hill School.

RIDE 35 *AMERICAN RIVER PARKWAY*

Change your mountain bike into an urban assault vehicle to explore the American River Parkway on the Jedediah Smith National Recreation Trail through Sacramento. The bike path is approximately 32.8 miles long, one way. I recommend that you consult your map, jump onto this path at any handy access point, and head out to Folsom Lake for a beautiful out-and-back ride. If you really are

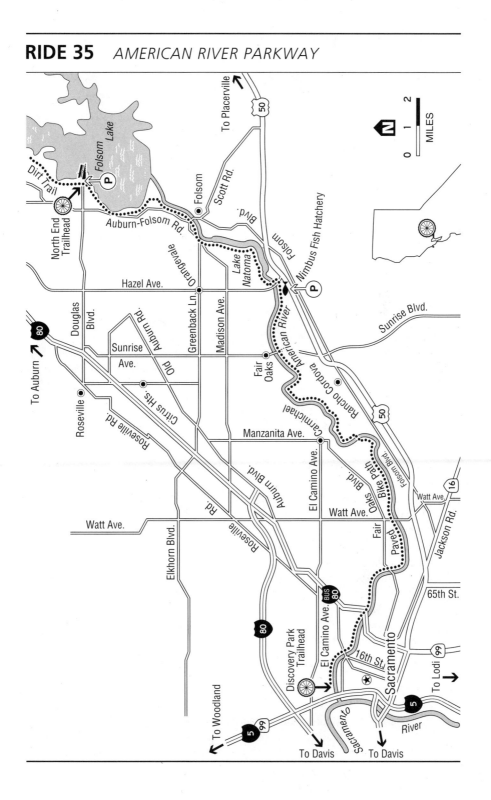

Riding along Folsom Lake where the Sacramento Bike Path turns to dirt.

yearning for some dirt, there's a short two-and-a-half-mile unpaved section at the end of the trail along Folsom Lake.

Despite its proximity to downtown Sacramento, the area surrounding the American River has maintained its natural appearance and displays a variety of landscapes, attracting an abundance of water birds. The northern portion of the ride follows the edge of Folsom Lake. Part of the trail is believed to have been built on a segment of the old Pioneer Express Trail, which linked the many mining camps that once lined the American River. The mining camps are now covered by man-made Folsom Lake, but many of their colorful names live on: Beals, Condemned, Long Horseshoe, Rattlesnake, and Oregon.

It may seem out of place to include a paved ride in a mountain bike guidebook, but a beautiful bike path like this one is hard to pass up. From Sacramento, the nearest unpaved mountain bike trails lie a fair distance to the east, in the Sierra, or to the west, in the coastal foothills. But along the American River Parkway, you can sample urban delights on a mountain machine.

General location: From downtown Sacramento to Folsom Lake, along the American River.

Elevation change: Sacramento's elevation is 25' and Folsom Lake's is 466'.

Season: This path offers fun riding throughout the year.

Services: All services are located in Sacramento.

Hazards: Take care to avoid collisions with other cyclists on this popular bikeway. Slow down when passing others on the path and let people know you're coming.

Rescue index: There is frequent traffic on the path so help is always near.

Land status: City, state, and national recreation land.

Maps: The *Sacramento Bicycle Commuter* map, free at most bike shops, shows the bikeway from Discovery Park to Folsom Lake, and also recommends the best routes for getting around town by bike.

Finding the trail: There are over 22 different access points within the first 20 miles of the bikeway. The *Sacramento Bicycle Commuter* map shows the many areas where car parking and access to the path are available. The path begins at Discovery Park, which is at the confluence of the American and Sacramento Rivers. To get there, take the Garden Highway exit off I-5 to Discovery Park Road and the park entrance. Park in the Discovery Park lot and look for a sign describing the path and a "Mile 0" sign. Mileage markers have been placed along the length of the bikeway.

Source of additional information: For more information, call the Sacramento County bicycle coordinator at (916) 440-5966.

Notes on the trail: Pick up the bikeway wherever is most convenient for you. The mileage signs along the way will give you an idea of where you are and how far you may want to go. Out-and-back rides are the easiest to arrange, but being dropped off at Folsom Lake and riding back into the city is also a possibility.

Lake Tahoe

RIDE 36 *THE FLUME (NEVADA)*

This 16-mile ride features spectacular views of Lake Tahoe. You'll either need to arrange a shuttle or pedal some extra road miles on NV 28 back to the trailhead. The first section of the ride is on gravel and dirt roads, but the actual Flume section is a narrow single-track with lots of exposure. If you have any fear of heights or cannot pick up your bike and climb over an obstacle, this ride probably isn't for you. After the narrow Flume section, the trail widens again to a broad dirt downhill. Late in the summer, the turns on this downhill section often become very sandy and very challenging to negotiate. On those really hot days, it feels great to jump into Lake Tahoe at the end of your ride.

The views on this ride feature breathtaking vistas of Lake Tahoe and the surrounding mountains, punctuated by the thrilling downhill descent. In addition, naturalists will appreciate the diverse forest including oak, cottonwood, aspen, ash, and birch, abundant birdlife, including nuthatches, chickadees, and flickers.

Local history also is interesting. Built in the 1800s, the Flume once carried water to the Nevada towns of Carson City and Virginia City. Today, remnants of the Flume are still visible on the trail. Fans of the Wild West might want to take a tour of the Ponderosa Ranch at the base of this ride. Please do not ride through the ranch on your bike; they prefer horses and charge a fee for tours.

General location: Approximately 12 miles south of Incline Village on the east side of Lake Tahoe.

Elevation change: The ride begins at Spooner Lake, elevation 7,100'. You'll climb to Marlette Lake at 7,823' and then drop down to Lake Tahoe at 6,200'. Total elevation gain is 1,300', with a total loss of 2,000'.

Season: Summer in the Lake Tahoe area is generally warm and dry. Occasionally, there are afternoon thundershowers so be sure and check the weather forecast. Temperatures can reach into the 90s during the day but the altitude sends them back down into the 40s by dusk. This is the classic Lake Tahoe ride and weekend use in the summer can be heavy, so plan accordingly. Fall is an ideal time to ride the Flume Trail because the crowds disappear after Labor Day and the trees display gorgeous fall colors. Be sure to carry extra layers for the cooler weather. Winter comes early, dusting the peaks with snow before Thanksgiving, and is

RIDE 36 *THE FLUME (NEVADA)*

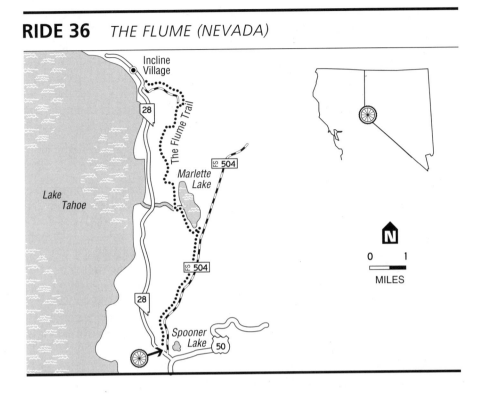

wet and cold. Spring arrives in May and the ground dries out quickly with the warmer weather.

Services: Water and rest rooms are available at Spooner Lake Park. Restaurants, groceries, and lodging are available in the nearby towns of South Lake Tahoe, Tahoe City, or Reno.

Hazards: The Flume Trail, where it traverses the hillside, is the most difficult section. It's a narrow trail and the steep hillside falls away to your left. The trail is badly eroded in some areas but repairs have been made, so riding is safe when done with a bit of caution. Nevertheless, this is not a good ride to do in bad weather or high winds.

On the final descent, the trail re-enters the trees. The trail is smooth here but watch your speed—occasional bumps can catch a rider unprepared.

Be prepared for sudden and sometimes dramatic weather changes at this high elevation. Dress in layers and carry raingear, even in summer.

Rescue index: During the summer, help might be available from people using this trail. Your likeliest other assistance would be located at either end of the ride, at the Ponderosa Ranch or by flagging down a car on NV 28.

Land status: Lake Tahoe Nevada State Park and Toiyabe National Forest.

Maps: See USGS topographic maps of Marlette Lake (7.5-minute series) and Carson City (15-minute series).

Finding the trail: This ride begins from the parking area at Spooner Lake Park (entrance fee is $3). The park is on the east side of Lake Tahoe, south of Incline Village and just west of the intersection of NV 28 with US 50. For the easier ride, use two cars; drop one north on NV 28 at Sand Harbor and drive the other one to Spooner Lake Park. Otherwise, you'll have approximately a 10-mile ride on NV 28 back to Spooner Lake Park.

Sources of additional information: Any of the bicycle shops in the Tahoe area will be familiar with the Flume ride.

Notes on the trail: From the north end of the Spooner Lake parking area, ride around the fire gate onto a dirt road. In about a third of a mile down the dirt road, turn left onto the main trail. The first 5 miles are on a smooth dirt road leading to Marlette Lake. At a bit less than 4 miles into the ride, stay left and begin the last steep ascent. From here, it's downhill to Marlette Lake.

Upon arriving at Marlette Lake, go left along the shore to the spillway at the southern end. Follow the single-track trail down the left side of the spillway outlet. About a tenth of a mile farther, turn right and cross the stream. Follow the trail up through the trees on the opposite side of the creek to the beginning of the Flume Trail. The initial quarter mile is narrow and tricky because of exposed tree roots, so you may want to walk parts of this stretch. However, the trail soon opens up and smoothes out, except for a few rocky areas where most riders dismount to avoid getting bounced off their bikes.

From the Flume Trail, turn left onto unmarked Tunnel Creek Road, which is a jeep road. Follow the long switchbacks down the hill until you reach a chain gate across the road that leads to Ponderosa Ranch. Turn left here; do not trespass onto ranch property. When you intersect with NV 28, turn left, and it's 1.5 miles back to Sand Harbor. You might want to reward yourself with a swim in Lake Tahoe, depending on the time of year.

RIDE 37 *TAHOE TO TRUCKEE (THE TNT)*

You can convert this approximately 20-mile one-way ride into a loop by riding CA 89 back to Tahoe City. (The highway is very busy but has a good shoulder.) The majority of this ride is on gravel fire roads, with the first segment on some smooth and easy-riding single-track. The most difficult section is the early six-mile climb to the summit; beyond the summit, you'll head mostly downhill to Truckee.

Although this beautiful ride parallels CA 89, you'll be high above the road,

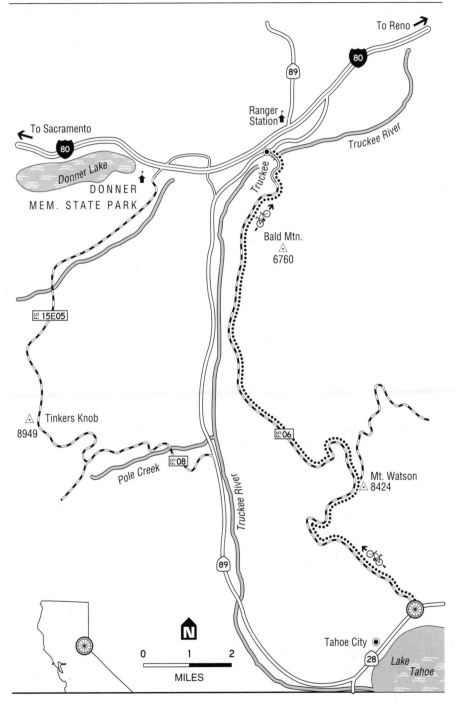

To Reno

80

89

Ranger
Station

Truckee River

To Sacramento

80

Donner Lake

DONNER
MEM. STATE PARK

Truckee

Bald Mtn.
△
6760

FS 15E05

Tinkers Knob
△
8949

FS 06

Mt. Watson
△ 8424

FS 08

Pole Creek

Truckee River

89

N

0   1   2

MILES

Tahoe City ⊙

28

Lake
Tahoe

away from any road noise. The views of the mountains are magnificent as you traverse the hillsides under Mount Watson and Sawtooth Ridge.

General location: Approximately 2 miles northwest of Tahoe City.˙
Elevation change: Starting at 6,000', this trail climbs to 7,650' before ending in Truckee at 5,856'. Total elevation gain is 1,650'; total loss is 1,800'.
Season: Late spring through early fall is the best time to ride, although you might want to avoid summer weekend crowds. Be prepared with raingear and warm clothing for the severe changes in temperature which can take place at this elevation.
Services: There's no water available on this ride so fill up before you leave Tahoe City, and carry plenty. Services are located on either end of the ride in Truckee or Tahoe City.
Hazards: At this high elevation, weather can change quickly. Dress in layers and carry warm clothing and raingear, even in summer, to protect yourself.
Rescue index: The closest help is in Truckee or Tahoe City.
Land status: Tahoe National Forest.
Maps: The Tahoe National Forest map is useful. For more detail, see the USGS 7.5-minute series topographic maps for Tahoe City or Truckee.
Finding the trail: From Tahoe City, drive approximately 1.5 miles east of town on CA 28. Turn left onto Old Mill Road, and continue a half mile to a T-intersection. Turn left there onto Polaris Road. In another half mile, the North Lake Tahoe High School will appear on your right. Park at the end of the high school parking lot. Your trail is the dirt road that begins at the end of Polaris Road, just to the left of the end of the parking lot.

Sources of additional information:

Paco's Truckee Bike & Ski
11200 Donner Pass Road
Truckee, CA 96161
(916) 587-5561

Olympic Bicycle Shop
620 North Lake Boulevard
Tahoe City, CA 95730
(916) 581-2500

Notes on the trail: Once on the trail, you'll soon pass a sign for Burton Creek Park. At the first intersection take a left; then take the next right. You'll go through two more intersections before your next turn. Meanwhile, you should be climbing gradually towards Antone Meadows with Burton Creek on your left. Turn right at the Y-intersection, about 2.3 miles into your ride. You'll easily identify this intersection by the state boundary sign facing the other direction. Take the single-track that climbs up and over to the main road. At the intersection with the main road, go right and continue climbing. However, before

The road from Tahoe to Truckee is a well-maintained gravel Forest Service road.

turning onto the main road, turn around for a fine view of Lake Tahoe. In another mile, you'll have reached the summit of this ride at 7,650'. Turn left at the Y-intersection and begin your descent on FS 06 to Truckee. Just beyond the Y-intersection is a green gate (for seasonal closure). A little more than a mile and a half from the gate, you'll encounter the two successive hairpin turns. A half mile beyond, a road will leave to the left for Deer Creek—stay right. There'll be a couple of short uphills but you'll cruise mostly down to Truckee. When you hit the pavement, turn left. Make the next right turn onto Silver Fir. Then turn left at the T-intersection onto Ponderosa Road. Follow this road down to CA 267, and turn left to go into Truckee.

RIDE 38 *BLACKWOOD CANYON*

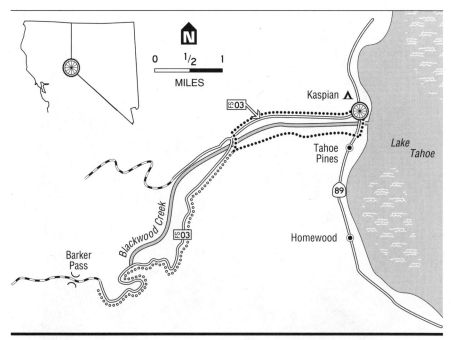

RIDE 38 *BLACKWOOD CANYON*

This easy eight-mile loop is a great beginner ride because it has very little elevation gain. As a bonus, there's a short, very smooth section that makes a good introduction to trail riding on a mountain bike. Novice riders will enjoy the manageable combination of paved road, wide dirt trail, and short gravel stretches.

If you'd like to add some miles, stay to your right at the junction just past Blackwood Creek, and head up into Blackwood Canyon. It's seven miles to the top of Barker Pass (1,500′ gain). To return, double back and pick up the short route back to the lake.

This is a wonderful early-morning ride because many birds are active then and are attracted to the water. Along Blackwood Creek, watch for chickadees, juncos, kingfishers, Clark's nutcrackers, Steller's jays, and blue herons among the cottonwood, willow, and aspen trees. Once on the bike path along Lake Tahoe, you might see Canada geese, California gulls, and various ducks.

Novice riders will enjoy the manageable Blackwood Canyon Trail.

General location: Four miles south of Tahoe City on CA 89.

Elevation change: The parking lot sits at 6300'. Total elevation gain on this ride is only 100'.

Season: Late spring through early fall brings the most pleasant riding, although midday and weekend traffic can be heavy on this ride. This ride is especially fun to do before breakfast, when the trails are less crowded and the animals are more active. Always be prepared for weather changes at this high altitude by carrying extra clothing.

Services: There are only rest rooms at the parking lot (no phones or water). North and south along CA 89 are many restaurants, groceries, motels, and camp-grounds. Tahoe City is just under 4 miles to the north.

Hazards: Always use caution when riding on a multi-use trail like this one. Watch and listen for hikers, horses, and other cyclists. Because this trail is so accessible, you may find it busy late in the afternoon and on weekends.

After finishing the main trail, be careful crossing over CA 89 to pick up the bike path back to the parking lot.

Rescue index: You're never far from assistance on this short ride; CA 89 is very close.

Land status: Tahoe National Forest and county roads.

Maps: Consult the Tahoe National Forest map and the USGS 7.5-minute series topographic map for Homewood.

Finding the trail: A little less than 4 miles south of Tahoe City on CA 89, turn right at Kaspian Park. Immediately after this turn, there's a driveway on your right leading to a parking lot, where this ride begins.

Sources of additional information:

Paco's Truckee Bike & Ski
11200 Donner Pass Road
Truckee, CA 96161
(916) 587-5561

Olympic Bicycle Shop
620 North Lake Boulevard
Tahoe City, CA 95730
(916) 581-2500

Notes on the trail: Turn right out of the parking lot onto the pavement. Follow the paved road for 2.4 miles until it veers left at a Y-intersection. (Do not follow the dirt road that goes straight.) Just beyond this junction, the paved road crosses Blackwood Creek. After the stream, watch for the trailhead. You'll be turning left onto a dirt road that is 5 to 6 feet wide. The dirt trail winds through the trees with some small ups and downs and occasional short gravel sections. About 1.4 miles down the trail, you'll see a green Forest Service gate; this gate might be closed but it's easy to get around.

The dirt trail soon returns to pavement, on a road called Grand Avenue. One half mile farther, Grand intersects with CA 89. Cross over CA 89 and turn left onto the bike path that parallels the highway back to Kaspian Park. After 1 mile, watch for your left-hand turn back into the parking area.

RIDE 39 *VERDI PEAK*

This beautiful 28-mile out-and-back features numerous scenic highlights. Except for one short downhill, it's mostly an uphill ride to the summit. The entire ride is on fire roads. The first half mile has two short paved sections; the second section is a short steep hill. The next ten miles cover a dirt road that generally is in good condition, although the steeper sections have some larger, loose rocks. Along the last three miles to the summit of Verdi Peak, you'll have to deal with some rough sections that are full of rocks. These sections are rideable, but riders frequently get off and walk them due to the combined effects of the altitude and the steep grade.

As you traverse this west-facing slope, natural splendor will unfold before you. Beginning at the lovely Boca Reservoir, you'll climb through forests of Douglas fir, cedar, and aspen. After the turnoff to Verdi Peak, there's a large grove of aspen, which is especially colorful in the fall. You'll also see a large basalt outcrop that resembles a castle. This appears to be the top, but climb on, because the true summit is approximately one mile farther, across a high alpine meadow that leads you into a large stand of Douglas fir. Here, the road ends at a trail that leads up to an abandoned fire tower. From this lookout on a clear day, you can see Reno, the Lake Tahoe basin, and the Boca and Stampede reservoirs.

As you ride, allow yourself time to stop, look, and listen, and you will discover abundant wildlife: chickadees, juncos, flickers, nuthatches, red-tailed hawks, ground squirrels, deer, and bears.

General location: Eight miles east of Truckee.

Elevation change: The ride begins at 5,600′ and climbs to the Verdi Peak fire lookout at 8,000′. Total elevation gain is 2,400′.

Season: Like all the Tahoe area rides, this one is best done in late spring to early fall. Be prepared for sudden weather changes with raingear and wool layers. The temperature can drop quickly and 14 miles can be a long way down.

Services: From the trailhead, it's 2 miles to a small gas station that has a pay phone and refreshments. Other services are available in Truckee.

Hazards: The downhill sections are plenty of fun, but be careful of large rocks and loose gravel.

Rescue index: The nearest phone is at the I-80 exit. If you need assistance, you might be 14 miles from help. Let someone know where you are going if you plan to ride alone.

Land status: Tahoe National Forest.

Maps: A Tahoe National Forest map is available at the local ranger station. For more detail, refer to the Truckee (15-minute series) or Boca (7.5-minute series) USGS topographic maps.

RIDE 39 *VERDI PEAK*

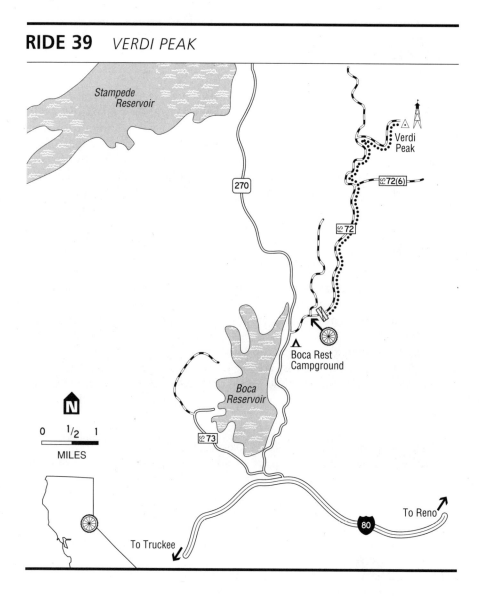

Finding the trail: From Truckee, take I-80 east for 6.5 miles to the Boca Reservoir/Hirschdale exit. Turn left onto the road towards Boca Reservoir. Your ride starts on a paved road just across from the Boca Rest campground, where a brown Forest Service sign posts the mileage to Verdi Peak (14 miles). Park your car in the campground or along the road to Verdi Peak.

Don't forget to stop and take in the great views from the top of Verdi Peak.

Sources of additional information:

Paco's Truckee Bike & Ski
11200 Donner Pass Road
Truckee, CA 96161
(916) 587-5561

Olympic Bicycle Shop
620 North Lake Boulevard
Tahoe City, CA 95730
(916) 581-2500

Notes on the trail: Turn right toward Verdi Peak onto the paved road across from the campground. At the top of a small rise, you'll see the brown sign for Verdi Peak. Then climb another short but very steep paved section. About a mile up, take the first right through the green gate, following FS 72. After this junction, do not turn off toward the right where a sign reads "FS 72 (6)," but instead stay on the main road, FS 72, which should be easy to follow. Continuing ahead, the main road drops downhill and then starts climbing slowly again. You'll see a Forest Service sign for Verdi Peak three miles to the right and Henness Pass straight ahead. Take the right toward Verdi Peak. Continue straight through a meadow. At the end of the road you are on is the trail that leads to the fire lookout, which has nearly a 360-degree view. Bring plenty of film along on this ride!

RIDE 40 *MARTIS PEAK*

If you like scenic overlooks, you'll like this eight-mile one-way climb with a fire lookout at the top. Little technical skill is required, due to good road surface, but you need to be a very strong rider to handle the climb. This ride is not a good choice for your first jaunt if you've just come up to this elevation; it's a tough uphill for 4.7 miles. If you can survive the first steep sections, the latter half of the ride seems a little easier. The road becomes more hardpack than gravel, and therefore feels a little smoother to ride on.

The road climbs through a dense Douglas fir forest where you can see flickers, nuthatches, juncos, ground squirrels, and deer. At the top, enjoy the view of the Truckee Valley from the old fire tower.

General location: About 8 miles southeast of Truckee, or just northwest of Kings Beach.

Elevation change: The dirt road begins at 7,100', just northwest of Brockway Summit. It then climbs to the top of Martis Peak, elevation 8,656'. Total elevation gain is 1,556'.

Season: Ride this one from late spring through early fall. As always bring a range of cold- and wet-weather gear; weather changes can be very extreme at this high altitude.

Services: For all services, go either to Truckee or Kings Beach.

Hazards: Bring enough water for this climb, which is short but steep—you'll need plenty of liquids.

Watch for other traffic on these roads.

Rescue index: Flagging down a motorist on CA 267 is your closest source of assistance.

RIDE 40 *MARTIS PEAK*

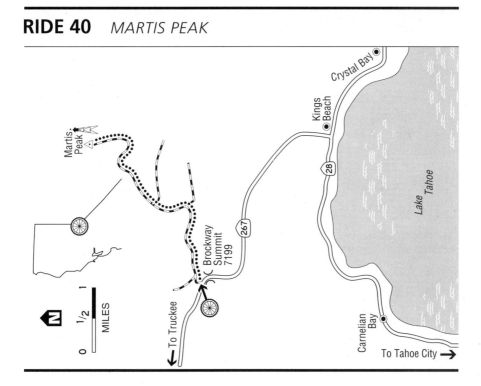

Land status: Tahoe National Forest.

Maps: The Tahoe National Forest map shows the road to Martis Peak, but not the many logging roads that branch off of it. For more detail, see the USGS 7.5-minute series map for Martis.

Finding the trail: The Martis Peak Road begins just north of Brockway Summit on CA 267. It isn't named but there's a stop sign at the entrance, which is very wide. You can park at the entrance or .3 miles up the road, in a wide turnaround spot with room for parking.

Sources of additional information:

Paco's Truckee Bike & Ski
11200 Donner Pass Road
Truckee, CA 96161
(916) 587-5561

Olympic Bicycle Shop
620 North Lake Boulevard
Tahoe City, CA 95730
(916) 581-2500

You'll be riding on old logging roads to the top of Martis Peak.

Notes on the trail: From the intersection with CA 267, stay left at the first rise. There will be three successive roads on the left that look like they could be the main road, but continue straight. This route will bring you to the top of Martis Peak. Enjoy your descent—you deserve it.

RIDE 41 *POLE CREEK*

On this 20-mile loop, you'll get a taste of several types of trails as you ride through the beautiful Tahoe scenery. The first half of the route is on wide gravel and dirt roads. A short, challenging single-track drops you down to Donner Lake and a paved road brings you back to the trailhead. Although I've described this ride as a loop, you can always shorten it to an out-and-back.

Pole Creek is the subalpine region of the Sierra Nevada. On this loop, you'll climb through pine forests and beautiful alpine meadows, which will sport

RIDE 41 *POLE CREEK*

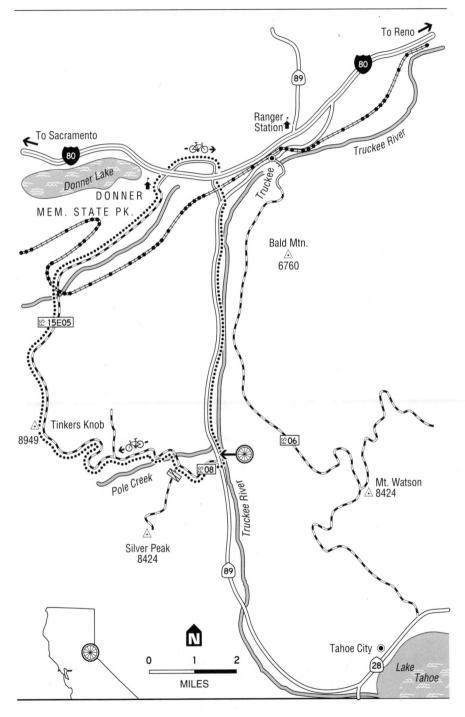

flowers in the spring and perhaps snow patches in the late fall. As you go up, you'll be rewarded with some terrific views of Silver Peak to the south and Sawtooth Ridge to the east.

Naturalists will enjoy glimpses of flickers, kinglets, nuthatches, woodpeckers, red-tailed hawks, ground squirrels, deer, and other wildlife along the way.

General location: Six and a half miles south of Truckee on CA 89.

Elevation change: CA 89 is at 6,040'. The bridge over Pole Creek sits at 6,560', and the intersection with FS 08 is at 7,280'. Upper Pole Creek dead-ends at around 7,600'.

Season: Late spring through early fall brings the best weather for riding this loop. Always be prepared with extra warm clothing and raingear for temperature changes, which can occur quickly at this elevation. Spring's highlights include the wildflowers carpeting the woods and meadows. In the fall, watch for the aspen turning golden yellow.

Service: There are no facilities on this loop. All services are available in Truckee or Tahoe City.

Hazards: The greatest hazard on this ride is not being prepared for the alpine climate, which can be severe even in summer. Always bring extra clothes and plenty of water.

Rescue index: Return to CA 89 and flag down a passing motorist.

Land status: Tahoe National Forest.

Maps: The Tahoe National Forest map, available at Donner Memorial State Park and at the Tahoe Ranger Station, doesn't show the road to upper Pole Creek. For more detail, see the USGS map for Tahoe City (7.5-minute series).

Finding the trail: From Truckee, take CA 89 south for approximately 6 miles. Turn right onto FS 08 across from Big Chief Lodge. Park your vehicle on the side of the road and begin your ride from here. From Tahoe City, it's about 7 miles north on CA 89.

Sources of additional information:

Paco's Truckee Bike & Ski
11200 Donner Pass Road
Truckee, CA 96161
(916) 587-5561

Olympic Bicycle Shop
620 North Lake Boulevard
Tahoe City, CA 95730
(916) 581-2500

Notes on the trail: From the intersection of CA 89 and FS 08, the paved portion of the road ends in .1 mile and turns into a two-lane gravel road. At the closed green gate on your left, you'll see a sign for FS 08 on your right. Continue on FS 08. Beyond the sign, there's a short downhill to a wooden bridge over Pole

Creek. After the bridge, the road goes left; follow it up the canyon. The next intersection is at the 3-mile mark. If you stay right, the road eventually dead-ends in 2 miles at a nice view of Deep Creek Canyon. If you go left, the road follows Pole Creek up into a beautiful meadow, looping around the meadow and underneath Tinkers Knob. Continue on the main trail as it wanders up and down. At the intersection with the signed Pacific Crest Trail, go right. This section drops down the south fork of the Coldstream Canyon on a challenging single-track that requires good bike handling skills. After you cross over the railroad tracks, it's mostly level riding through Donner Memorial State Park, Truckee, and on CA 89 back to your starting point at FS 08.

Bridgeport

RIDE 42 BRIDGEPORT RESERVOIR TO CHEMUNG MINE

This is a ten-mile out-and-back on a wide gravel road, that climbs uphill the whole way out at various degrees of difficulty. The first part of the ride is a gentle climb; then the road switchbacks up the hill. A little past the one-and-a-quarter-mile mark, there's a cattleguard, consisting of parallel metal bars that cross the road, with a ditch underneath. You may want to dismount and walk your bike here.

In wet weather, sections of the fire road get very muddy, so it's best to avoid this ride after a heavy rain. Washboard bumps occur along certain stretches; watch for these on the descent.

This ride starts at the edge of Bridgeport Reservoir, which is used for boating and fishing when water levels allow. The surrounding area is high desert, and the desert bloom makes this ride a recommended choice for early spring. Few trees grow here other than the aspen.

The sweeping grassland and Bridgeport Reservoir offer beautiful views. Nevertheless, the highlight of this ride is the old Chemung Mine. A former gold mine, it was closed in the 1950s and slowly is falling down. You can wander through it and see the interesting old machinery that was left behind. From the mine site, there's a stunning view of the snowcapped Sierra Nevada peaks.

General location: Just under 4 miles north of Bridgeport.
Elevation Change: The ride begins at 6,457′ and climbs to 8,122′. Total elevation gain and loss is 1,665′.
Season: Late spring to early fall is the best time to ride in this area. In early spring, you may see some desert bloom amid hints of green, although the trail may be quite muddy from snowmelt. In late summer and fall, the vegetation will be brown and dry. In September, note the aspens turning brilliant yellow.
Services: There are no facilities on the trail. All services are available in Bridgeport.
Hazards: Bring plenty of water and warm clothing for this ride.

If you're uncomfortable riding across the cattleguard, be careful when walking your bike. This road is also used by others who want to see the mine, so watch and listen for trucks.

At the mine, use extreme caution if you explore the building interior. Heavy snow, wind, and rain have damaged the structure and most of it is unsound.

RIDE 42 *BRIDGEPORT RESERVOIR TO CHEMUNG MINE*

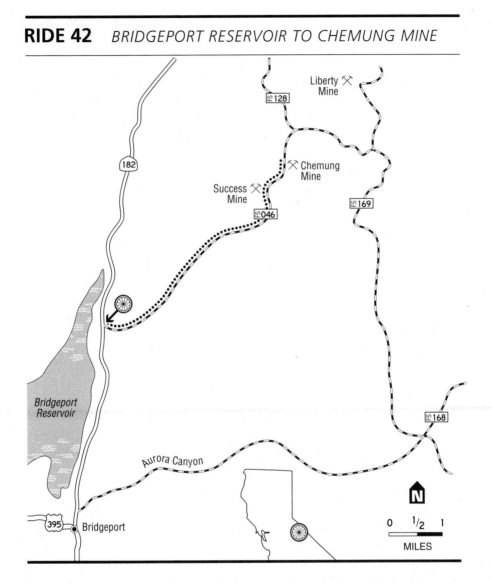

On the return trip, go slow on the descent and watch for washboard bumps.
Rescue index: The Chemung Mine is 5.3 miles from CA 182. There are several homes on the highway along the reservoir where you could stop for assistance.
Land status: Bureau of Land Management and Toiyabe National Forest.
Maps: The Toiyabe National Forest map shows this route very clearly and is available at the Bridgeport Ranger Station, just south of Bridgeport on US 395. The USGS topographic map of Bridgeport (7.5-minute series) also shows this route.

The Chemung Mine is just one of the many defunct mines around Bridgeport.

Finding the trail: Take CA 182 north of Bridgeport for 3.8 miles. On the right will be a paved entrance to a dirt fire road, FS 046. It has a stop sign facing the other way. You may park your car in the pulloff just inside the entrance to this road.

Source of additional information:

> Bridgeport Ranger District
> Toiyabe National Forest
> P.O. Box 595
> Bridgeport, CA 93517
> (619) 932-7070

Notes on the trail: From CA 182 it's 1.3 miles up FS 046 to the cattleguard. The road climbs another 2.9 miles until it begins to level out. On your left, you'll see an old mine shaft and some scattered debris from the Success Mine. Continue on ahead for another mile and the Chemung Mine will be on your right. After you've explored the mine, return the way you came. If you'd like a longer workout, the fire road continues on for many miles through the hills.

Mono Lake

RIDE 43 *BLACK POINT*

This short ten-mile out-and-back on a wide gravel road has beautiful views of Mono Lake and a fun rock structure to explore at Black Point. The road is mostly level and well maintained for car traffic.

Mono Lake is an ancient inland sea, twice the size of San Francisco and three times as salty as the ocean. This unique lake drains seven streams that wash salts and minerals off the eastern slope of the Sierra Nevada. However, Mono Lake has no outlet and the water evaporates, leaving the salt behind. Despite the salty, alkaline water, the lake attracts more than 80 species of migratory birds, including grebes, phalaropes, and snowy plovers. An estimated 90 percent of the California gull population nests here each spring. These birds eat the brine shrimp and the brine fly that live on the algae that grows in the lake. The Mono Lake shrimp, fly, and algae are uniquely adapted to this lake and exist nowhere else. Unfortunately, this delicate ecosystem was threatened in 1941 when the city of Los Angeles started diverting four of the seven streams for its municipal water supply. Since then, Mono Lake has doubled in salinity and the water level has dropped approximately 40 feet. Efforts have been underway for the past few years to try to find practical solutions to the problems faced by this ecosystem.

The valley and surrounding peaks have been shaped by volcanic activity through millions of years. Black Point is the result of a volcanic eruption that began beneath the lake about 13,000 years ago. At that time, Mono Lake was some 400 feet deeper than it is today. As the top of Black Point cooled, it contracted and narrow fissures formed at the summit, which you can now explore if you hike up. Give yourself an hour and a half (three miles round-trip) to climb Black Point.

General location: Just 4.3 miles north of Lee Vining.
Elevation change: The parking area at Mono County Park is at 6,461' and the parking area at Black Point is at 6,463'. In between, there is very little elevation gain or loss.
Season: The high elevation of this area limits its seasonable use. Winters are very cold and wet. Spring often comes late, with June being the first month without snowfall. Summers are dry and hot, with occasional thunderstorms in the after-

noon. September and October generally are ideal for riding because the daytime temperatures are cooler and most of the summer tourist traffic is over.

Services: At Mono County Park, you'll find shade, water, rest rooms, and a large grassy area with picnic tables, but no phones. All other services are located in Lee Vining. Be sure to visit the Mono Lake Visitor Center in town for a complete selection of books, maps, and brochures.

Hazards: Use caution when sharing the road with motorists, and be sure to move over to the right if traffic approaches.

If you hike up Black Point, be careful when exploring the fissures.

Rescue index: Rangers sometimes patrol this area. If you need assistance, the nearest sure source of help is Lee Vining.

Land status: Mono Lake Tufa State Reserve and Mono Basin National Forest Scenic Area.

Maps: A map of the Mono Lake Tufa State Reserve is available for 50¢ from either of the following addresses (see "Sources of additional information"). You can also use the USGS 7.5-minute quads for Lundy and Negit Island.

Finding the trail: From Lee Vining, drive 4.3 miles north on US 395. Turn right and drop down into Mono County Park. Park your car in the lot by the picnic area.

Sources of additional information:

Mono Lake Tufa State Reserve
P.O. Box 99
Lee Vining, CA 93541
(619) 647-6331

Mono Basin National Forest Scenic Area
P.O. Box 429
Lee Vining, CA 93541
(619) 647-6525

Notes on the trail: From the parking lot at Mono County Park, continue down the road. After a mile, you'll see the Mono Lake Cemetery on your right and the pavement ends. Two-tenths of a mile farther, stay left where the road coming in on the right has a "Keep Out" sign. Just past a small stream, turn right towards Black Point. It's 2 miles from here to the turnaround. If you want to hike up Black Point, lock your bike in the parking lot. The climb to the summit is 500' high and takes about an hour and a half one-way. Returning to the Black Point parking lot, retrace your route to Mono County Park.

RIDE 43 *BLACK POINT*
RIDE 44 *SOUTH TUFA LOOP*

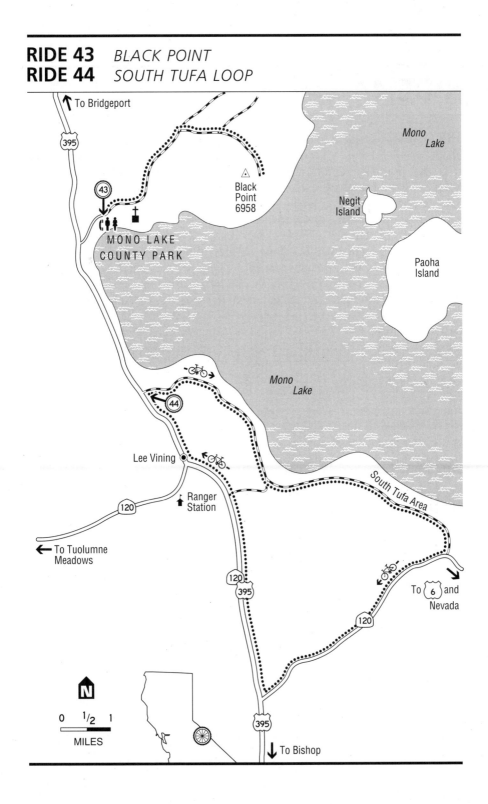

To Bridgeport

395

43

MONO LAKE
COUNTY PARK

Black
Point
6958

Mono
Lake

Negit
Island

Paoha
Island

Mono
Lake

44

Lee Vining

South Tufa Area

Ranger
Station

120

To Tuolumne
Meadows

120
395

To 6 and
Nevada

120

N

0   1/2   1

MILES

395

To Bishop

RIDE 44 *SOUTH TUFA LOOP*

This is another scenic ride along the shore of Mono Lake, and a chance to get up close and personal with the unique formations of tufa (deposits of porous rock) that dominate the landscape. It can be done as an out-and-back ride of 14 miles on two-wheel-drive roads, or if you'd like to do a loop of approximately 18 miles, you can connect with a paved road back to the marina. The first mile is on a rough single-lane gravel road that connects with an improved dirt road. From that intersection, it's another seven miles to the South Tufa area on a two-lane gravel road. This road has some washboard bumps and can be very dusty with passing cars. If you choose to do the loop instead of riding back on the gravel, follow signs to CA 120. It's well under a half mile from the South Tufa area until you turn right onto the pavement to return to Lee Vining.

General location: Two miles north of Lee Vining on US 395.
Elevation change: There is very little elevation change along the lake. If you do the loop ride, there's a total elevation change of 300'.
Season: September and October are the best months to ride this loop. Daytime temperatures are cool yet comfortable, and most tourists have gone home. Summer temperatures can be very hot, with possible afternoon thunderstorms. During the rest of the year, access to the Mono Lake region from the west may be closed by snow, even as late as May.
Services: There's no water at the parking area, so fill your bottles before the ride. All services are located in Lee Vining. Be sure to visit the Mono Lake Visitor Center in downtown Lee Vining for a complete selection of books, maps, and brochures.
Hazards: Be sure to carry enough water; it can get very hot and dry on this loop in the summer.
Rescue index: You're seldom far from assistance if you stay on these roads. There often are rangers at the marina and South Tufa parking lots.
Land status: Mono Lake Tufa State Reserve and Mono Basin National Forest Scenic Area.
Maps: A map of the Mono Lake Tufa State Reserve is available for 50¢, from either of the following addresses (see "Sources of additional information") and in the marina parking lot. You can also use the USGS 7.5-minute quads for Lundy and Negit Island.
Finding the trail: From Lee Vining, drive 3 miles north on US 395. Turn right and go down into the marina parking area. Park your car here. It's a good idea to carry a lock to secure your bike at the South Tufa area.

Sources of additional information:

Mono Lake Tufa State Reserve
P.O. Box 99
Lee Vining, CA 93541
(619) 647-6331

Mono Basin National Forest Scenic Area
P.O. Box 429
Lee Vining, CA 93541
(619) 647-6525

Notes on the trail: Starting at the marina, Mono Lake will be on your left as you ride to the South Tufa formations. Within a half mile, you'll see a large dark tufa formation that looks like a cave. It was formed when this land was still under ancient Mono Lake, but it's slowly eroding so please don't climb on it. You'll see many similar formations near and in the lake as you pedal along. Once at the South Tufa area, lock up your bike and walk the footpath through the formations, which have many markers explaining the development of tufa and also giving some history. Once back on your bike riding towards US 395, you can marvel at Mono Craters, the moonscape on your left.

NEVADA

Carson City

RIDE 45   *BRUNSWICK CANYON AND THE VIRGINIA & TRUCKEE RAILROAD*

This ride can be adapted for all abilities—you can cover from eight to ten miles, all on gravel or half on pavement if ridden as a loop. You can add miles by exploring the various quarries along the route. The gentle grade and beautiful scenery along the river highlight this excursion. The first mile is well maintained because it leads to a quarry, but beyond, the surface becomes rough as the road follows the Carson River while it meanders through the valley.

Historical sites line this route. The Virginia & Truckee (V & T) Railroad once serviced the mills along the Carson River. These mills processed ores from the Virginia City mines.

General location: Just east of Carson City, off US 50.
Elevation change: The ride starts at 4,611' with the highest point being 4,900'.
Season: It's possible to ride in this area any time of the year. However, keep in mind that summers are hot and dry, and this ride offers little in the way of shade. Fall brings the best weather, with cool daytime temperatures. Winters are cold but you can have a great ride if you dress in layers. Spring brings desert flowers but sometimes the roads can be muddy.
Services: All services are located in Carson City. For a full-service bike shop, go to Capitol Bicycles.
Hazards: Use extreme caution when exploring the old mill sites; many of them are very unstable.
Rescue index: US 50 would be your closest source of assistance.
Land status: County roads.
Maps: Any city or county map of the Carson City area.
Finding the trail: From Carson City, go east on US 50. Turn right onto Deer Run Road and park on the side of the road just before crossing the Carson River. From here, you can see the gravel road that follows the river going into the canyon.

Sources of additional information:

Bentley Brooks
Capitol Bicycles
900 North Carson Street
Carson City, NV 89701
(702) 883-3210

RIDE 45 *BRUNSWICK CANYON AND THE VIRGINIA & TRUCKEE RAILROAD*

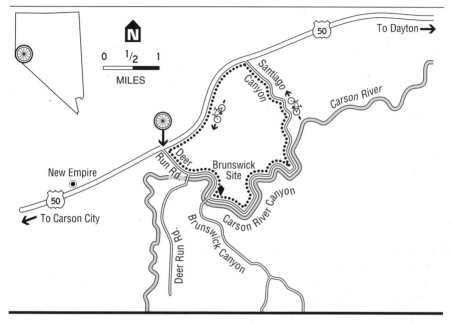

Notes on the trail: During the first mile of the ride, look in the river and you can see the remains of old diversion dams used by the early stamp mills. After a mile, there's a bridge on the right that leads into Brunswick Canyon. One of the supports for the bridge was the turntable at Mound House. If you look closely, you can see the V & T Railroad builder's plate. Do not cross the bridge, but continue to veer to the left around the quarry and along the river. As you pass the quarry, you'll be able to see some stone foundation work, all that remains of the Brunswick Mill. As you travel on, looking across the river, you'll see another old mill site that makes a nice side trip. (Simply cross the turntable bridge; then follow the road along the other side of the river.)

Returning to the main route, you'll pass the remains of another large mill, and then the grade will begin its gradual climb up the canyon toward Mound House. The spectacular view down the canyon reveals several points where dirt roads lead down to the river. If you watch as you climb, you may see the rotting remains of ore bins that served mills down in the canyon.

Finally you'll turn away from Carson River Canyon and enter Santiago Canyon. If you look carefully down Carson River Canyon, you can see the remains of the roadbed for the little 1-mile Eureka Mill Railroad, which also makes an interesting side trip. If you stay on the roadbed, you'll come out on US 50 at Mound

House. At one time, this was an important interchange between the V & T Railroad and the Carson & Colorado Railroad. You have several options here: turn onto US 50 and return to Carson City on pavement, return the way you came, or continue through Mound House toward Virginia City on the historic route of the V & T.

Note: Information on this ride was collected and written by Bentley Brooks and William Mobley.

Great Basin National Park

RIDE 46 *WHEELER PEAK*

This is a very tough out-and-back ride up and down Wheeler Peak. The road is paved, narrow, and steep. You'll gain 3,000 feet over the 12 miles from the Visitor Center to the end of the Peak road. But the downhill is great. Please note that mountain biking is allowed only on designated motor vehicle roadways. The park has miles of dirt roads, but you must ask a ranger which ones are open.

On October 27, 1987, the former Great Basin National Monument was designated a national park in recognition of the unique beauty of the Great Basin. The park encompasses the Snake range of Nevada, although the Great Basin actually includes most of the state and portions of Oregon, Idaho, Utah, Wyoming, and California. What sets this land apart is that its rivers have no drainage to the sea (hence the name, "Great Basin"). The characteristic Basin topography is a series of valleys and mountain ranges all running roughly north and south. Many of the valleys start at elevation 6,000' and some mountains rise to 13,000'.

Wheeler Peak has several zones of vegetation that are representative of the Great Basin. Pinyon pine, juniper, and Mormon tea begin to cover the mountain slopes at 6,000'. Above 8,000', the woodland is more complex, with limber pine and quaking aspen. You'll also find Engelman spruce and other varieties of pine. Many animal species also live in this area; the most common creature is the jack rabbit. Other small rodents such as kangaroo rats, mice, and ground squirrels often will be seen around the campfire as they come looking for crumbs. Mountain lions and bobcats live here too, but they're hard to spot. The bighorn sheep have been pushed back into the remote areas and are rarely seen.

At 13,061', Wheeler Peak is the highest summit in Great Basin National Park. On its flanks grow the world's oldest living species of tree, the ancient bristlecone pine. The oldest known specimen was dated at 4,900 years of age when it was cut down. At the base of the mountain is the only surviving glacier in the Great Basin region. And a ranger-guided tour of the cave will show you this park's underground attractions.

General location: A little over 6 miles west of Baker.
Elevation change: Lehman Cave, your starting point, is at 6,800'. You'll climb to Wheeler Peak Campground at 10,000' for a total gain of 3,200'.
Season: March through early October are the months when riding without snow

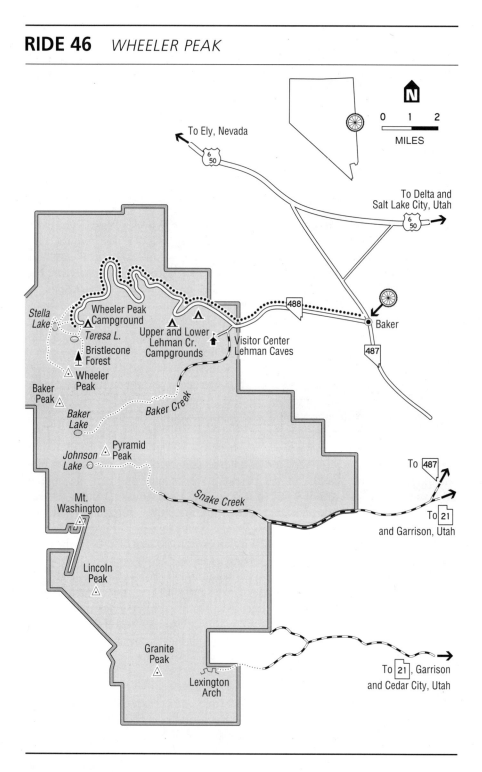

is possible. The warmest months are June through September. Because of this area's high elevation, nighttime temperatures can get very cold, even in summer. Fall is a beautiful time to ride, as the aspen turn yellow and orange, and the Oregon grape adds splashes of red.

Services: Telephones, water, and rest rooms are available at the Visitor Center. Baker, a very small town, is the nearest source of groceries, gas, and a meal. For greater selection, try Ely, 62 miles from Baker. There are 6 campgrounds located in the park. Inquire at the Visitor Center for site availability, and for a listing of commercial facilities in Baker and Ely.

Hazards: Watch for car traffic; this road is narrow and can get very busy during the summer.

You'll need to carry plenty of water, since it's easy to become dehydrated at this elevation.

Rescue index: Return to the Visitor Center for assistance.

Land status: National park.

Maps: The Visitor Center has a free map that serves as a general guide to the park. For more detail, the six 7.5-minute series USGS maps that cover this area are Windy Peak, Lehman Caves, Wheeler Peak, Kious Spring, Minerva Canyon, and Arch Canyon. These topographic maps are all available through the Great Basin Natural History Association, Baker, NV 89311. The Humboldt National Forest map also includes Great Basin National Park.

Finding the trail: From Baker, take NV 488 west to Great Basin National Park. In 5 miles, the road splits; take the left fork to Lehman Caves and the Visitor Center. Park your car there for a tour of the caves and to ride up Wheeler Peak.

Sources of additional information:

Great Basin National Park
Baker, NV 89311
(702) 234-7331

Great Basin Natural History Association
Baker, NV 89311

As of this writing, all bicycles are prohibited on trails or roads that are not open to motorists. It has been indicated to me that some old roads may be designated for bicycle use in the future. Please inquire at the Visitor Center for current information.

Las Vegas

RIDE 47 *BRISTLECONE TRAIL*

This beautiful five-mile loop ride in the hills above Lee Canyon offers a dramatic change of scenery from the valley floor of Las Vegas. Sagebrush gives way to thick stands of trees as you climb towards Mount Charleston. These forests are composed of ponderosa pine, white fir, bluebell, snowberry, penstemon, and much more. Above the Bristlecone Trail on the slopes of Mount Charleston grow bristlecone pines, which were established here 4,000 years ago (making these trees older than the redwoods or even the giant sequoias).

Not only is this loop a lovely mountain bike ride, but the drive up and back to Las Vegas is interesting as well. To get to Lee Canyon you can drive through Kyle Canyon, a narrow beautiful canyon that cuts in towards the Spring Mountains, of which Mount Charleston is the tallest peak. If you have the time, stop at the Cathedral Rock picnic area in Kyle Canyon and take the one-mile hike to Cathedral Rock for a great view of the canyon. Back on the road to Lee Canyon (north on NV 158), watch for a sign to the Desert View Trail, another short hike with a beautiful view. Turn left into Lee Canyon, where there are several campgrounds and the Lee Canyon ski area. After your ride, you can take NV 156 back to US 95 to return to Las Vegas instead of backtracking through Kyle Canyon.

General location: Forty-six miles northwest of Las Vegas.
Elevation change: It's a 680' climb from the trailhead at 8,671' to the trail summit.
Season: This is a great place to escape the summer heat. At this high elevation, the temperature will be several degrees cooler than in Las Vegas. In the winter, this area is a ski resort so the snowfall dictates how early in the spring you may ride the trails. Your best bet is late spring through early fall.
Services: Bring food and water from Las Vegas; some supplies and lodging are available at the Mount Charleston Resort in Kyle Canyon. Camping is available in Lee Canyon.
Hazards: This trail has the usual hazards of mountain bike trails: ruts, rocks, and roots.
Rescue index: The ranger station in Kyle Canyon (off NV 157) is a good source of assistance spring through fall.
Land status: Toiyabe National Forest (Las Vegas Ranger District).

RIDE 47   *BRISTLECONE TRAIL*

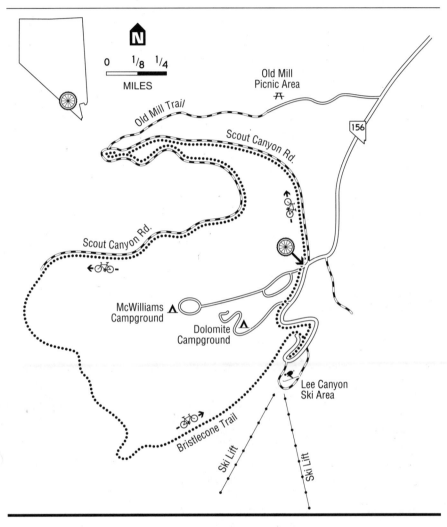

Maps: The Toiyabe National Forest map shows this route in the Las Vegas Ranger District.

Finding the trail: There are two options to get to the trailhead. For the most direct route, take US 95 north out of Las Vegas for 54 miles and turn left onto NV 156 to Lee Canyon. For the sightseeing option take US 95 north out of Las Vegas for 20 miles and turn left onto NV 157 to Kyle Canyon, then turn right onto NV 158 then left into Lee Canyon. Follow the road back into the canyon.

As the paved road goes right, just past the Clark County Youth Camp, watch for a dirt road on your right. This is the Scout Canyon Road; look for the signpost. Park your car in the pullout.

Sources of additional information:

> Bikes West
> 6162 West Spring Mountain Road
> Las Vegas, NV 89102
> (702) 873-3372

Notes on the trail: The trail starts out as Scout Canyon fire road, which climbs gently to the trail summit, about 3 miles into the ride. Here the road becomes the single-track Bristlecone Trail. This trail is level for about one-quarter of a mile, drops about 50 meters, then levels out for a short stretch until it drops down a small valley to the Lee Canyon Ski Area. Watch for the ski lifts off to your right. Once back on the pavement you are in the ski area parking lot; find your way back out to the main road and you will pass your car.

Note: Information on this ride was collected by Jim Barlow.

RIDE 48 *RED ROCK HILLS*

This 15-mile loop winds through the desert on a paved, one-way, double-wide road that allows plenty of passing room. You'll be happy you're on a mountain bike when you encounter gravel on the pavement, where the road crosses washes. This scenic ride offers beautiful views of the Red Rock Hills, also known as the Spring Mountain Range and the Wilson Cliffs. The hills are composed of ancient ocean deposits now seen as gray limestone and sandstone that have been reddened by iron oxide. Along the loop there are many worthwhile areas to stop and explore if you so desire. One such place is Lost Creek Canyon, where there's a seasonal waterfall. Most of these sites involve a short hike, so bring along a lock to secure your bike at the trailhead.

Desert plant life is more abundant here than in Las Vegas. The Red Rock Canyon Recreation Lands area is 2,000' to 5,000' higher and gets up to a foot more rain per year. Common plants to look for include several kinds of cacti: cholla, barrel, prickly pear, and beaver tail. Small shrubs abound, such as sage, yucca, and agave. There also are many varieties of small trees, depending on the availability of water, such as ponderosa pine, pinyon pine, cedar, willow, and manzanita. Numerous birds, rodents, and reptiles live here. Watch for hawks, eagles, falcons, roadrunners, owls, ravens, and wrens. There's a good chance you'll see squirrels, lizards, and rattlesnakes as well. Dusk and early morning are the best times to spot animals that are trying to avoid the heat.

RIDE 48   *RED ROCK HILLS*

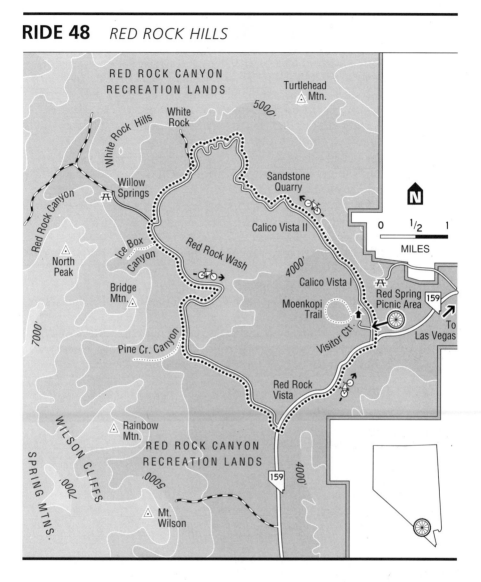

Be sure to stop in and explore the Visitor Center, which has wonderful geological and historical displays. If you enjoy this Visitor Center you'll also want to check out the one at Spring Mountain Ranch, which was owned at different times by many interesting people, including Chester Lum, the "Lum" of the old "Lum and Abner" radio show and Vera Krupp, wife of German munitions industrialist Alfred Krupp von Bohlen und Halbach, before being sold to the Nevada Division of State Parks. It is just south on NV 160.

General location: Twenty-five miles west of Las Vegas.

Elevation change: The ride starts at 3,700′ and climbs to 4,700′ before descending back to 3,700′. Total elevation gain is 1,000′.

Season: This road is accessible year-round. Spring and fall offer the best scenery and weather. Summer months are so hot that riding should only be done early in the day. Besides, sudden and severe thunderstorms may pop up on summer afternoons. In winter, you might find some snow at the top.

Services: All services are located in Las Vegas. For water, rest rooms, and phones, return to the Red Rock Visitor Center (open daily 9 A.M. to 4 P.M.).

Hazards: As mentioned earlier, watch out for gravel on the pavement around road cuts and at intersections with secondary roads and washes. Also watch for falling rock off the road cuts.

Bring plenty of water, then bring a little bit more. No water is available on the loop. This can be an extremely hot ride, and the air usually is very dry. If you do any hiking watch out for rattlesnakes.

Rescue index: You're never far from help on this ride because it's a popular scenic area close to Las Vegas.

Land status: Bureau of Land Management.

Maps: The map supplied free at the Visitor Center is excellent and also mentions interesting facts about the park.

Finding the trail: From downtown Las Vegas, take Charleston Street west towards Red Rock Canyon. Park at the Red Rock Canyon Visitor Center. Start your ride by turning left out of the Visitor Center onto the one-way scenic loop.

Sources of additional information:

Bikes West
6162 West Spring Mountain Road
Las Vegas, NV 89102
(702) 873-3372

Red Rock Canyon Recreation Lands
Bureau of Land Management
Las Vegas, NV 89126
(702) 363-1921

Notes on the trail: Starting at the scenic drive entrance, the road climbs 1,000′ in the first 5 miles. The undulating grades will test your gearing skills, but after the switchbacks at the top, the ride back down is quick. Be careful to keep your speed under control.

RIDE 49   POTOSI PASS

This is a five- to ten-mile loop on gravel and dirt roads, with several options for varying the length and difficulty of the ride. It's 2.5 miles to Potosi Pass, then another 1.5 miles to Potosi Spring. From the spring it's just another mile to the old Potosi Mine, which was one of the original (1850s) Mormon lead mines.

The road climbs to Potosi Pass, getting steeper close to the summit. If you choose to continue on to Potosi Spring, the road descends 530 feet, which you'll have to make up on the return to NV 160. From the spring to the Potosi Mine, the road becomes steeper and rougher on this last mile—you may want to walk, or take the challenge.

This gravel road is used to access several camps, and therefore is well maintained, but dust from passing cars can be a problem in the summer months. Near the top, traction gets harder to find but you can usually find a smooth line to follow. You'll be traveling through a forest of mesquite trees which doesn't offer much shade. In summer, plan to ride early or late in the day when there'll be shady spots along the road.

General location: Twenty miles southwest of Las Vegas.

Elevation change: The road starts at 5,073' and climbs to 6,243' at Potosi Pass. It drops to 5,710' at Potosi Spring.

Season: Late spring and early fall are the best seasons for this ride, especially if you want to avoid the heat. The winter months are also rideable, but you're likely to encounter snow. Summer can get too hot for riding, but at this elevation, you'll be 10 to 20 degrees cooler than down in Las Vegas. Ride early or late in the day to avoid the heat and catch a little shade.

Services: There are no facilities on the trail. For local refreshments, there's a bar located at Mountain Springs Summit, approximately 8 miles farther west on NV 160. All other services are located in Las Vegas.

Hazards: As always in this arid region, carry plenty of water. Watch out for other vehicles using this road, especially when on the descent. Keep your speed under control.

Rescue index: During the summer there are people staying in the camps along the road. If you cannot find any one at these camps, it's best to return to NV 160.

Land status: Bureau of Land Management.

Maps: Refer to the USGS topographic maps for Potosi and Cottonwood Pass (7.5-minute series).

Finding the trail: Take I-15 south out of Las Vegas. Turn onto NV 160 west at Exit 33. From this exit, it's 20 miles to the Potosi Pass road. Watch for a green sign on the right that says "BSA Camp" and "Mount Potosi next left." Turn left

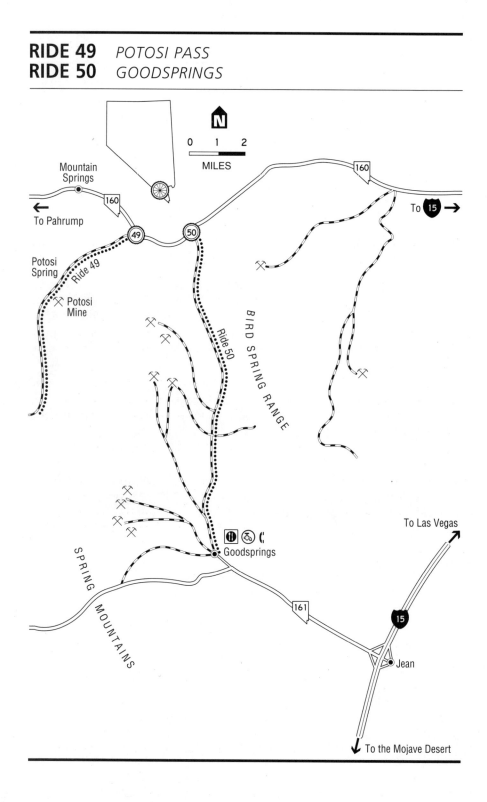

onto the gravel road and park next to the large green sign shaped like the state of Nevada.

Sources of additional information:

Bikes West
6162 West Spring Mountain Road
Las Vegas, NV 89102
(702) 873-3372

Note: Information on this ride was collected by Jim Barlow.

RIDE 50 *GOODSPRINGS*

This is a 26-mile ride out-and-back to the town of Goodsprings. Because the route is mostly level, with very few hills, the greatest adversity you're likely to encounter is heat or wind. The entire ride travels a gravel and dirt road on which technical skill is not as important as endurance.

The landscape is classic desert, dominated by many types of cacti, sage, mesquite, and brittlebush. If you want shade, perhaps a Joshua tree might do. You won't see much animal activity unless you ride early in the morning or at dusk, but you may see an occasional burro, turkey vulture, or rabbit.

Goodsprings is an old mining town founded in 1856. Stop to read the historic marker as you come into town on Reverse Street. Be sure to visit the Pioneer Saloon for a cold drink and some shade. This place has a history of its own, including a few bullet holes in the wall from a past Hell's Angels visit. Never fear, it still makes a great rest stop halfway through the ride. If someone in your group gets tired, he or she can always wait at the Pioneer Saloon to be picked up later on your return trip.

General location: Sixteen miles west of Las Vegas.
Elevation change: The trail starts at 4,200', climbs to 4,920' at Cottonwood Pass, and drops to Goodsprings at 3,700'.
Season: Year-round riding is available on this road. The desert in bloom is subtle but spectacular; watch for cactus blossoms in March and April. Spring and summer days can get very hot, so get an early start and carry plenty of water. Winter can be very cold yet rewarding if you dress appropriately. You can always get a hot drink in Goodsprings.
Services: The Pioneer Saloon is open from 10 A.M. to 10 P.M. seven days a week. They serve drinks, pizza, burritos, and nachos. All other services are located in Las Vegas.
Hazards: Burro droppings may decorate the road, so use those bike handling

skills to avoid them. If you see any burros, do not feed or try to pet them. They're wild and best left to themselves.

Rescue index: People in Goodsprings can be of assistance, or return to NV 160. The highway is well traveled and someone will be along shortly.

Land status: Bureau of Land Management.

Maps: This route appears on the USGS topographic maps for Cottonwood Pass and Goodsprings (7.5-minute series).

Finding the trail: Take I-15 south out of Las Vegas. Turn west at Exit 33 onto NV 160, and drive 16 miles. Watch for a "slippery when wet" sign on the right; approximately .1 mile later, you'll see a dirt road on the left that leads off into the desert. There's a dirt pulloff on the right-hand side where you can park your car.

Sources of additional information:

Bikes West
6162 West Spring Mountain Road
Las Vegas, NV 89102
(702) 873-3372

Notes on the trail: This gravel road runs south between two mountain ranges and remains mostly level with just a few rolling hills. There are a few access roads to mines up in the hills but the main road is easy to distinguish from these smaller side roads. Traffic is limited to a few trucks and motorbikes. On your way back to NV 160 you will encounter a fork in the road; take the road on the right. The left branch goes up into the hills of the Spring Mountains.

Note: Information on this ride was collected by Jim Barlow.

Afterword

LAND-USE CONTROVERSY

A few years ago I wrote a long piece on this issue for *Sierra* magazine that entailed calling literally dozens of government land managers, game wardens, mountain bikers, and local officials to get a feeling for how riders were being welcomed on the trails. All that I've seen personally since, and heard from my authors, indicates there hasn't been much change. We're still considered the new kid on the block. We have less of a right to the trails than horses and hikers, and we're excluded from many areas, including:

a) wilderness areas
b) national parks (except on roads, and those paths specifically marked "bike path")
c) national monuments (except on roads open to the public)
d) most state parks and monuments (except on roads, and those paths specifically marked "bike path")
e) an increasing number of urban and county parks, especially in California (except on roads, and those areas specifically marked "bike path")

Frankly, I have little difficulty with these exclusions and would, in fact, restrict our presence from some trails I've ridden (one time) due to the environmental damage and chance of blind-siding the many walkers and hikers I met up with along the way. But these are my personal views. The author of this volume and mountain bikers as a group may hold different opinions.

You can do your part in keeping us from being excluded from even more trails by riding responsibly. Many local and national off-road bicycle organizations have been formed with exactly this in mind, and one of the largest—the National Off-Road Bicycle Association (NORBA)—offers the following code of behavior for mountain bikers:

1. I will yield the right-of-way to other non-motorized recreationists. I realize that people judge all cyclists by my actions.
2. I will slow down and use caution when approaching or overtaking another cyclist and will make my presence known well in advance.
3. I will maintain control of my speed at all times and will approach turns in anticipation of someone around the bend.
4. I will stay on designated trails to avoid trampling native vegetation

Some trails need 24 to 48 hours to recover from a recent rain.

and minimize potential erosion to trails by not using muddy trails or short-cutting switchbacks.

5. I will not disturb wildlife or livestock.
6. I will not litter. I will pack out what I pack in, and pack out more than my share whenever possible.
7. I will respect public and private property, including trail use signs and no trespassing signs, and I will leave gates as I have found them.
8. I will always be self-sufficient and my destination and travel speed will be determined by my ability, my equipment, the terrain, the present and potential weather conditions.
9. I will not travel solo when bikepacking in remote areas. I will leave word of my destination and when I plan to return.
10. I will observe the practice of minimum impact bicycling by "taking only pictures and memories and leaving only waffle prints."
11. I will always wear a helmet whenever I ride.

Now, I have a problem with some of these—number nine, for instance. The most enjoyable mountain biking I've ever done has been solo. And as for leaving word of destination and time of return, I've enjoyed living in such a way as to

A friendly reminder that mountain bikers should yield to both hikers and horses.

say, "I'm off to pedal Colorado. See you in the fall." Of course it's senseless to take needless risks, and I plan a ride and pack my gear with this in mind. But for me number nine smacks too much of the "never-out-of-touch" mentality. And getting away from civilization, deep into the wilds, is, for many people, what mountain biking's all about.

All in all, however, NORBA's is a good list, and surely we mountain bikers would be liked more, and excluded less, if we followed the suggestions. But let me offer a "code of ethics" I much prefer, one given to cyclists by Utah's Wasatch-Cache National Forest office.

Study a Forest Map Before You Ride
Currently, bicycles are permitted on roads and developed trails within the Wasatch-Cache National Forest except in designated Wilderness. If your route crosses private land, it is your responsibility to obtain right of way permission from the landowner.

Keep Groups Small
Riding in large groups degrades the outdoor experience for others, can disturb wildlife, and usually leads to greater resource damage.

Avoid Riding on Wet Trails
Bicycle tires leave ruts in wet trails. These ruts concentrate runoff and accelerate erosion. Postponing a ride when the trails are wet will preserve the trails for future use.

Stay on Roads and Trails
Riding cross-country destroys vegetation and damages the soil.

Always Yield to Others
Trails are shared by hikers, horses, and bicycles. Move off the trail to allow horses to pass and stop to allow hikers adequate room to share the trail. Simply yelling "Bicycle!" is not acceptable.

Control Your Speed
Excessive speed endangers yourself and other forest users.

Avoid Wheel Lock-up and Spin-out
Steep terrain is especially vulnerable to trail wear. Locking brakes on steep descents or when stopping needlessly damages trails. If a slope is steep enough to require locking wheels and skidding, dismount and walk your bicycle. Likewise, if an ascent is so steep your rear wheel slips and spins, dismount and walk your bicycle.

Protect Waterbars and Switchbacks
Waterbars, the rock and log drains built to direct water off trails, protect trails from erosion. When you encounter a waterbar, ride directly over the top or dismount and walk your bicycle. Riding around the ends of waterbars destroys them and speeds erosion. Skidding around switchback corners shortens trail life. Slow down for switchback corners and keep your wheels rolling.

If You Abuse It, You Lose It
Mountain bikers are relative newcomers to the forest and must prove themselves responsible trail users. By following the guidelines above, and by participating in trail maintenance service projects, bicyclists can help avoid closures which would prevent them from using trails.

I've never seen a better trail-etiquette list for mountain bikers. So have fun. Be careful. And don't screw up things for the next rider.

Dennis Coello
Series Editor

Glossary

This short list of terms does not contain all the words used by mountain bike enthusiasts when discussing their sport. But it should serve as an introduction to the lingo you'll hear on the trails.

ATB	all-terrain bike; this, like "fat-tire bike," is another name for a mountain bike
ATV	all-terrain vehicle; this usually refers to the loud, fume-spewing three- or four-wheeled motorized vehicles you will not enjoy meeting on the trail—except, of course, if you crash and have to hitch a ride out on one
bladed	refers to a dirt road that has been smoothed out by the use of a wide blade on earth-moving equipment; "blading" gets rid of the teeth-chattering, much-cursed washboards found on so many dirt roads after heavy vehicle use
blaze	a mark on a tree made by chipping away a piece of the bark, usually done to designate a trail; such trails are sometimes described as "blazed"
BLM	Bureau of Land Management, an agency of the federal government
buffed	used to describe a very smooth trail
catching air	taking a jump in such a way that both wheels of the bike are off the ground at the same time
clean	while this may describe what you and your bike *won't* be after following many trails, the term is most often used as a verb to denote the action of pedaling a tough section of trail successfully
deadfall	a tangled mass of fallen trees or branches
diversion ditch	a usually narrow, shallow ditch dug across or around a trail; funneling the water in this manner keeps it from destroying the trail
double-track	the dual tracks made by a jeep or other vehicle, with grass or weeds or rocks between; mountain bikers can ride in either of the tracks, but you will of course find that whichever one you choose, and no matter how many times you

change back and forth, the other track will appear to offer smoother travel

dugway a steep, unpaved, switchbacked descent

feathering using a light touch on the brake lever, hitting it lightly many times rather than very hard or locking the brake

four-wheel-drive this refers to any vehicle with drive-wheel capability on all four wheels (a jeep, for instance, has four-wheel-drive as compared with a two-wheel-drive passenger car), or to a rough road or trail that requires four-wheel-drive capability (or a *one*-wheel-drive mountain bike!) to negotiate it

game trail the usually narrow trail made by deer, elk, or other game

gated everyone knows what a gate is, and how many variations exist upon this theme; well, if a trail is described as "gated" it simply has a gate across it; don't forget that the rule is if you find a gate closed, close it behind you; if you find one open, leave it that way

Giardia shorthand for *Giardia lamblia,* and known as the "back-packer's bane" until we mountain bikers expropriated it; this is a waterborne parasite that begins its life cycle when swallowed, and one to four weeks later has its host (you) bloated, vomiting, shivering with chills, and living in the bathroom; the disease can be avoided by treating (purifying) the water you acquire along the trail (see "Hitting the Trail" in the Introduction)

gnarly a term thankfully used less and less these days, it refers to tough trails

hammer to ride very hard

hardpack used to describe a trail in which the dirt surface is packed down hard; such trails make for good and fast riding, and very painful landings; bikers most often use "hardpack" as both a noun and adjective, and "hard-packed" as an adjective only (the grammar lesson will help you when diagramming sentences in camp)

jeep road, a rough road or trail passable only with four-wheel-drive
jeep trail capability (or a horse or mountain bike)

kamikaze while this once referred primarily to those Japanese fliers who quaffed a glass of saki, then flew off as human bombs in suicide missions against U.S. naval vessels, it has more recently been applied to the idiot mountain bikers who, far less honorably, scream down hiking trails, endangering the physical and mental safety of the walking, biking, and equestrian traffic they meet; deck guns were necessary to stop the Japanese kamikaze pilots, but a bike pump or walking staff in the spokes is sufficient for the current-day kamikazes who threaten to get us all kicked off the trails

multi-purpose   a BLM designation of land which is open to many uses; mountain biking is allowed

out-and-back   a ride where you will return on the same trail on which you pedaled out; while this might sound far more boring than a loop route, many trails look very different when pedaled in the opposite direction

portage   to carry your bike on your person

quads   bikers use this term to refer both to the extensor muscle in the front of the thigh (which is separated into four parts) and to USGS maps; the expression "Nice quads!" refers always to the former, however, except in those instances when the speaker is an engineer

runoff   rainwater or snowmelt

signed   a "signed" trail has signs in place of blazes

single-track   a single, narrow track through grass or brush or over rocky terrain, often created by deer, elk, or backpackers; single-track riding is some of the best fun around

slickrock   the rock-hard, compacted sandstone that is *great* to ride and even prettier to look at; you'll appreciate it even more if you think of it as a petrified sand dune or seabed, and if the rider before you hasn't left tire marks (from unnecessary skidding) or granola bar wrappers behind

snowmelt   runoff produced by melting snow

snowpack   unmelted snow accumulated over weeks or months of winter—or over years in high-mountain terrain

spur   a road or trail that intersects the main trail you're following

technical   terrain that is difficult to ride due not to its grade (steepness) but to its obstacles—rocks, logs, ledges, loose soil . . .

topo   short for topographical map, the kind that shows both linear distance *and* elevation gain and loss; "topo" is pronounced with both vowels long

trashed	a trail that has been destroyed (same term used no matter what has destroyed it . . . cattle, horses, or even mountain bikers riding when the ground was too wet)
two-wheel-drive	this refers to any vehicle with drive-wheel capability on only two wheels (a passenger car, for instance, has two-wheel-drive); a two-wheel-drive road is a road or trail easily traveled by an ordinary car
water bar	An earth, rock, or wooden structure that funnels water off trails to reduce erosion
washboarded	a road that is surfaced with many ridges spaced closely together, like the ripples on a washboard; these make for very rough riding, and even worse driving in a car or jeep
wilderness area	land that is officially set aside by the federal government to remain *natural*—pure, pristine, and untrammeled by any vehicle, including mountain bikes; though mountain bikes had not been born in 1964 (when the United States Congress passed the Wilderness Act, establishing the National Wilderness Preservation system), they are considered a "form of mechanical transport" and are thereby excluded; in short, stay out
wind chill	a reference to the wind's cooling effect upon exposed flesh; for example, if the temperature is 10 degrees Fahrenheit and the wind is blowing at 20 miles per hour, the wind-chill (that is, the actual temperature to which your skin reacts) is *minus 32* degrees; if you are riding in wet conditions things are even worse, for the wind-chill would then be *minus 74 degrees!*
windfall	anything (trees, limbs, brush, fellow bikers) blown down by the wind

A native of Portland, Oregon, AIMÉE SERRURIER has enjoyed a long history of cycling. Her bike-touring career began in grade school when she joined her parents on a tour down the West Coast during the bicentennial. Mountain biking became her avocation before her graduation from Colorado College, where she also organized and participated in many rides and tours. Aimée came to the San Francisco Bay area to be a bicycle tour guide for Backroads, Inc. While with Backroads, she led trips in North America, Mexico, and France. Aimée still finds time to explore old and new rides in northern California while working full time as a registered nurse in San Francisco. This is her first book.

DENNIS COELLO'S AMERICA BY MOUNTAIN BIKE SERIES

Happy Trails

Hop on your mountain bike and let our guidebooks take you on America's classic trails and rides. These "where-to" books are published jointly by Falcon Press and Menasha Ridge Press and written by local biking experts. Twenty regional books will blanket the country when the series is complete.

Choose from an assortment of rides—easy rambles to all-day treks. Guides contain helpful trail and route descriptions, mountain bike shop listings, and interesting facts on area history. Each trail is described in terms of difficulty, scenery, condition, length, and elevation change. The guides also explain trail hazards, nearby services and ranger stations, how much water to bring, and what kind of gear to pack.

So before you hit the trail, grab one of our guidebooks to help make your outdoor adventures safe and memorable.

Call or write
Falcon Press or Menasha Ridge Press
Falcon Press
P.O. Box 1718, Helena, MT 59624

1-800-582-2665

Menasha Ridge Press
3169 Cahaba Heights Road, Birmingham, AL 35243
1-800-247-9437

Menasha Ridge Press

FALCONGUIDES *Perfect for every outdoor adventure!*

FISHING
Angler's Guide to Alaska
Angler's Guide to Montana

FLOATING
Floater's Guide to Colorado
Floater's Guide to Missouri
Floater's Guide to Montana

HIKING
Hiker's Guide to Alaska
Hiker's Guide to Alberta
Hiker's Guide to Arizona
Hiker's Guide to California
Hiker's Guide to Colorado
Hiker's Guide to Florida
Hiker's Guide to Georgia
Hiker's Guide to Hot Springs
  in the Pacific Northwest
Hiker's Guide to Idaho
Hiker's Guide to Montana
Hiker's Guide to Montana's
  Continental Divide Trail
Hiker's Guide to Nevada
Hiker's Guide to New Mexico
Hiker's Guide to North Carolina
Hiker's Guide to Oregon
Hiker's Guide to Texas
Hiker's Guide to Utah
Hiker's Guide to Virginia
Hiker's Guide to Washington
Hiker's Guide to Wyoming
Trail Guide to Glacier/Waterton
  National Parks
Wild Country Companion

MOUNTAIN BIKING
Mountain Biker's Guide to Arizona
Mountain Biker's Guide to
  Central Appalachia
Mountain Biker's Guide to Colorado
Mountain Biker's Guide to New Mexico
Mountain Biker's Guide to Northern
  California/Nevada
Mountain Biker's Guide to Northern
  New England
Mountain Biker's Guide to the
  Northern Rockies
Mountain Biker's Guide to the Ozarks

Mountain Biker's Guide to
  the Southeast
Mountain Biker's Guide to
  Southern California
Mountain Biker's Guide to Southern
  New England

ROCKHOUNDING
Rockhound's Guide to Arizona
Rockhound's Guide to Montana

SCENIC DRIVING
Arizona Scenic Drives
Back Country Byways
California Scenic Drives
Colorado Scenic Drives
New Mexico Scenic Drives
Oregon Scenic Drives
Scenic Byways
Scenic Byways II
Trail of the Great Bear
Traveler's Guide to the Oregon Trail
Traveler's Guide to the
  Lewis and Clark Trail

WILDLIFE VIEWING GUIDES
Arizona Wildlife Viewing Guide
California Wildlife Viewing Guide
Colorado Wildlife Viewing Guide
Florida Wildlife Viewing Guide
Idaho Wildlife Viewing Guide
Indiana Wildlife Viewing Guide
Montana Wildlife Viewing Guide
Nevada Wildlife Viewing Guide
New Mexico Wildlife Viewing Guide
North Carolina Wildlife Viewing Guide
North Dakota Wildlife Viewing Guide
Oregon Wildlife Viewing Guide
Tennessee Wildlife Viewing Guide
Texas Wildlife Viewing Guide
Utah Wildlife Viewing Guide
Washington Wildlife Viewing Guide

PLUS—
Birder's Guide to Montana
Hunter's Guide to Montana
Recreation Guide to
  California National Forests
Recreation Guide to Washington
  National Forests